Group's emergency Response
handbook
for DISASTER RELIEF

Group

Loveland, Colorado
group.com

Group resources actually work!

This Group resource incorporates our R.E.A.L. approach to ministry. It reinforces a growing friendship with Jesus, encourages long-term learning, and results in life transformation, because it's

Relational
Learner-to-learner interaction enhances learning and builds Christian friendships.

Experiential
What learners experience through discussion and action sticks with them up to 9 times longer than what they simply hear or read.

Applicable
The aim of Christian education is to equip learners to be both hearers and doers of God's Word.

Learner-based
Learners understand and retain more when the learning process takes into consideration how they learn best.

Group's Emergency Response Handbook for Disaster Relief

Copyright © 2009 Group Publishing, Inc.

Visit our website: **group.com**

Credits
Chief Creative Officer: Joani Schultz
Senior Editor: Jan Kershner
Copy Editor: Ann Jahns
Book Designer/Print Production Artist: Pamela Poll Graphic Design
Cover Art Director/Designer: Jeff A. Storm
Illustrator: Pamela Poll
Production Manager: DeAnne Lear

Unless otherwise indicated, all Scripture quotations are taken from the *Holy Bible*, New Living Translation, copyright © 1996, 2004. Used by permission of Tyndale House Publishers, Inc., Carol Stream, IL 60188. All rights reserved.

The names and identifying information of individuals who shared their stories have been changed.
This book is not to be considered the final authority on any of these topics, and should not be considered legal advice.

Library of Congress Cataloging-in-Publication Data

Group's emergency response handbook for disaster relief / [contributing authors, Robert E. Bagley ... et al.].
    p. cm.
ISBN 978-0-7644-3746-5 (pbk. : alk. paper)
1. Church work with disaster victims. 2. Disaster relief. 3. Social service–Religious aspects–Christianity. I. Bagley, Robert E. II. Title: Emergency response handbook for disaster relief.
HV554.4.G76 2009
363.34'575–dc22
                                2009009037

10 9 8 7 6 5 4 3 2 1   17 16 15 14 13 12 11 10 09

Printed in Canada.

om 1-Bookshelf 1-Shelf 5-47

oup's Emergency Response Handbo

u: **3HZAF70006OV**

ryGood

markings observed to text. Ships quick. Securely pac
shipped.

ip To

m A. Willem
6 PERRY HALL BLVD APT 304
TTINGHAM, MD 21236-1317

der Details

ler ID   114-7562058-5467461
ler Date   8/5/2019 3:34:48 PM
pping Service   Standard
vers Name   Brian A. Willem

Bengal Books strives to have each an
very customer 100% satisfied with th
purchase. If for any reason you are n
100% satisfied please email us at
rlacinak@cox.net with your concern
Like us on FACEBOOK at BENGAL
BOOKS.

f we need to make something right, v
will, <u>Guaranteed!</u>

MANY THANKS TO OUR TALENTED AUTHORS:

Major Robert E. Bagley, The Salvation Army, Supplies and Purchasing Secretary, U.S.A. Southern Territory

Gary W. Carr, Th.Div., D.Min., Chaplain Corps, US Navy (ret), Deputy Chief Chaplain, Colorado State Patrol

Jennifer S. Cisney, M.A., CRT, Team Coordinator, AACC Christian Crisis Response program

Rev. Dr. Kevin L. Ellers, D.Min., Territorial Disaster Services Coordinator for The Salvation Army in the U.S.A. Central Territory, president of the Institute for Compassionate Care

Sues Hyde, Director of Outreach, International Bible Society

Gina Leuthauser, M.S.W.

Mike Orfitelli, Territorial Disaster Services Coordinator, The Salvation Army

Major Bert Tanner, Territorial Director for KROC Center Development, The Salvation Army

Contents

Introduction

It's not easy losing a loved one in an accident. Or surviving a terrorist attack. Or losing your home in a flood or tornado. It's hard and painful and brutal.

Survivors of disasters and crisis situations should never have to face trials on their own. Those around them—particularly their Christian brothers and sisters—should rise up and support them.

"Share each other's burdens, and in this way obey the law of Christ" (Galatians 6:2).

Although it isn't easy going through trials, it's also tough being on the outside and trying to help those who are suffering. You don't know what to do. You want desperately to step in and alleviate some of the pain, but you're not sure how to begin, and you don't want to say the *wrong* thing.

Group's Emergency Response Handbook for Disaster Relief will help you come alongside those who are facing tough times after a disaster or crisis event. From care and counseling tips, to practical ministry ideas, to what to say and what not to say, this book offers insight into how to care for the hurting.

Of course, it'd be great if you never had to pick up this book! But the reality is that crisis events and disasters happen. Everyone faces tough times—those who share the Christian faith, as well as those who are unchurched or adhere to other religious beliefs. And they need your help.

So, when someone you know is recovering after a natural disaster or terrorist attack, suffering from depression, dealing with a financial crisis, or considering suicide…it's time to pick up this guide. Use the table of contents to find the specific hurt for which you're caring, and then flip to that section.

Once there, you'll find a **real-life narrative,** a story from someone who's been there. Sometimes they're inspiring, and you'll read how the support and love of a caring group sustained a person through a hard time. Other times they're disappointing and tell stories of people left alone during tragedy or rejected during trial. Either way, these stories will move you and show you the importance of being there for others.

Each section also includes **care and counseling tips** that will give you practical ideas for reaching out in love. From just listening to arranging for services, these ideas will help you effectively support those who are coping with the effects of a disaster or crisis.

Next you'll find **ministry tips.** These practical ideas will enable you to share your faith in meaningful and helpful ways.

And finally, you'll find an invaluable section on **what to say and what not to say.** The words we use can help or hurt more than we know. This section will help you avoid the hurtful comments and use the helpful ones.

You'll also find a useful box in each section that offers **Scripture help,** plus **referral guidelines** for referring survivors to a professional counselor. In addition, you'll find guides to additional resources such as helpful books and websites. Finally, a disaster response gear checklist will help you prepare to set out to offer your services.

Our prayer for this book is that it will help you help others through the difficult times following disaster or crisis.

—Major Robert E. Bagley, The Salvation Army, Supplies and Purchasing Secretary, U.S.A. Southern Territory

The names and identifying information of the people who have shared their stories have been changed.

The information in this book is meant to be a guide to help you respond effectively in the aftermath of a disaster or crisis. This is not professional advice meant to replace that which you would receive from professional personnel or licensed counselors and psychologists.

CHAPTER ONE

Crisis of Faith
Supporting Those Who Doubt

The strong winds that blow over the Continental Divide in the Colorado Rockies usually blow storms quickly through Estes Park out to the Front Range. But the winds on July 31, 1976 were unusually weak. A storm system had gathered above the Big Thompson Valley and remained stationary for almost three hours. More than 8 inches of rain dumped into the canyon below Estes Park. The sheer rock of the canyon couldn't absorb much water and channeled the downpour into a 19-foot wall of water that pushed 10-foot boulders, cars, and campers effortlessly down the canyon.

Sharon was meeting at Sylvan Dale Guest Ranch with 34 other women who served as leaders in an international missionary organization. The guest ranch sits in a lovely valley just east of the mouth of the Big Thompson Canyon. The group was surprised to hear sirens. Their surprise turned to fear as a police officer with a bullhorn directed them to evacuate. And fear gave way to panic as the officer urgently directed them to run.

The ladies knew they had to get to higher ground, but few knew which way to go to find it. Two of the cars followed a police officer toward the nearby city of Loveland. The road descended toward the river. The women approached a stretch of road covered with water and attempted to venture through. The first car stalled just as the wall of water pushed the car into the river. Two of the women in the two cars clung to trees until they were rescued. The other seven perished.

Sharon remained at the ranch. A man led her and the remaining group of ladies up the hills to higher ground. They were later joined by others who shared the news of the loss of their friends and co-workers.

When Sharon first learned of the fate of her friends, she was devastated and brokenhearted. All seven of the women were in their early 20s. She soon found herself questioning God—asking why he would bring them all together for a wonderful reunion—only to have it end in such a tragic way.

"God, why did you let this happen to me? Why did you have me come from California to be caught in a flash flood? Don't you know how much I love you?" Sharon's questions nagged at her heart as she tried to deal with the loss of her friends, and she desperately groped to find meaning in the midst of a senseless tragedy. The most difficult question of all shook Sharon to the core: "Why did you take them, God, and not me?"

More than 130 people lost their lives in the Big Thompson flood. Sharon tried to be thankful that she was alive, to look at the heroism of the rescue workers, and to think of the countless people who survived while their property was destroyed. But the grief of the situation caused her to focus on those who lost their lives rather than to be thankful for the majority who were rescued or spared.

Sharon's shaken but enduring faith in God gave her the strength to move through grieving. And the strength and support of the ladies who mourned with her helped her through the beginning steps of emotional healing. She found herself reliving the horror of the experience, but by giving it all over to God she was able to thank him for bringing her through safely. As she worked through the events and emotions of the disaster, her depression began to lift.

Through reading the Bible, Sharon realized that God wanted her to give thanks *in the middle of this disaster*, and other crises that might come, and learn to fully trust him. Prior to her experience, she had believed the Bible was telling her to be thankful *for* everything that happened in her life. However, she discovered that it is not about giving thanks *for* every circumstance in her life but rather *in the middle of everything that happens in her life.* Since that time, when she catches herself questioning difficult circumstances, she said she finds the peace of God in her heart by remembering how much he loves her.

SCRIPTURE HELP

+ **Deuteronomy 7:9**
+ **Psalm 33:4**
+ **Psalm 36:5**
+ **Psalm 100:5**
+ **Psalm 145:13**

+ **Proverbs 3:5**
+ **Isaiah 26:4**
+ **Matthew 6:28-30**
+ **1 Thessalonians 5:24**
+ **1 Peter 1:8-9**

Care and Counseling Tips

THE BASICS

A person's beliefs about justice, safety, and the trustworthiness of others are shaped by the circumstances of his or her experience. A person who has spent decades in relative security and safety may feel the world is more or less just, life is primarily secure, and disaster is found in other places. When disaster strikes, it becomes impossible to view the world in the same way.

The person who has gone through disaster is forced to re-examine the ideas and beliefs that bolstered his or her sense of security. Long-held beliefs about God are by no means exempt from this examination. Some of these beliefs may have been erroneous from the beginning. For example, a person may have believed that God does not allow disaster and pain to harm his children. Other held beliefs are true but are difficult to accept in the wake of disaster. For instance, a person may have previously believed that God is good, but struggles now that he or she has personally endured so much suffering.

While intellectual difficulties and arguments are a central part of a person's crisis of faith, a faith crisis usually stems from an emotional pain or loss. A person who has suffered a disaster may feel that God has broken trust in some way, wronged him or her, or simply callously refused to extend protection and grace. A person's deep anger, hurt, or disappointment in God may be expressed through intellectual objections to God's character, promises, or nature.

Care Tips

+ Commit to remain connected.

When a person deliberately turns or slowly slips away from faith in Christ, he or she almost always pulls back from the influences and people who support faith in Jesus. The faith community and the people who are a part of it are the earthly representatives of the God who has become difficult to accept or find. This may stem, in part, from the community's inability to embrace the person in the midst of his or her difficult questions or "negative" attitude. Remember that isolation is the Enemy's primary weapon in dragging people away from the faith.

Disaster survivors need others to stick by them more than they need the right answers to the tough questions, more than they need to be challenged for faulty thinking, and more than they need standard Christian responses. Friends and family don't have to agree with everything the survivor says, but sticking by no matter what he or she says is a vital part of healing after a disaster.

Encourage those working with the survivor not to be surprised when the survivor fails to return phone calls or to welcome meeting. Have them commit to remain connected no matter how the survivor responds.

+ Validate and listen to questions.

You may feel intimidated, afraid, or deeply concerned when a disaster survivor starts revealing his or her faith struggles. But as Solomon said, "There is nothing new under the sun." The victim is struggling with the same questions of pain and suffering that humans have always struggled with. Don't agree with statements that contradict Scripture, but do your best to empathize with the survivor's perspective. God can handle honest questions.

+ Look for productive outlets for the disaster survivor's grief and pain.

Work through a book on grief together, or go through a book on Christian apologetics, such as *Mere Christianity* by C.S. Lewis. Encourage the person to join a grief recovery group. Also explain the importance of talking with a Christian counselor or pastor to deal with the anger and disappointment he or she may feel toward God.

+ Pray with and for the disaster survivor.

You can't change what happened. But God has the power to bring comfort, healing, joy, and restoration to any victim's heart. Help the person take the big questions and disappointments directly to God in prayer. Ultimately, he or she will have to work out this faith crisis with God. Encourage the person to get in the habit of talking to God.

There is a deeper faith waiting for the survivor on the other side of grief. However, there is a risk that the person may not be able to make it through. And the simple truth is that he or she cannot make it through without God's help. So pray for the person, constantly asking God to help the person emerge with a deeper relationship with Jesus.

Counseling Tips

Ministering to an individual in the midst of a crisis of faith can be difficult. These tips can help.

+ Bring survivors back to the basics.

In the midst of the survivor's confusion, it's important to help him or her find spiritual anchors to hold on to. Avoid forcing or suggesting truths he or she *should* believe. Instead draw out of the person what he or she knows to be true. For example, the survivor may have new and significant questions about the love of God, but at the same time may be certain that God exists.

The survivor may be tempted to pick and choose parts of faith that feel like a better fit for current emotions. By bringing the person back to foundational truths, you can help him or her move past some of the questioning and back to a faith that transcends momentary feelings. The truths that weather this storm will be the foundation of an unshakeable faith in the future.

+ Provide multiple opportunities for the survivor to share accounts of the ordeal.

It's likely that at least part of the survivor's crisis of faith stems from the emotional hurt and trauma experienced as a result of the disaster. The person can begin to work through the trauma by sharing his or her story multiple times. The disaster survivor will find that new details and perspectives emerge with each retelling of the story. The most effective help you can offer is reserving judgment and providing a safe place for him or her to share.

Avoid the temptation to offer trite solutions or responses. Instead, share the person's burden through empathy, and ask for opportunities to pray together in the midst of the hurt.

Ministry Tips

+ Rally around the church members and people in your community who have been affected.

This is the chance to be the church in action. In the wake of a disaster, people are usually more than willing to help—they just don't know what to do. You don't have to solve the entire problem or even meet the greatest need. Think about the needs you have seen in the life of the survivor you are working with, and enlist the help of local churches to meet that need. For example, if the food in the survivor's refrigerator has gone bad, quickly launch a fridge restock drive. Fill the victim's refrigerator up and the refrigerators of neighbors who have been affected.

Nothing helps a person through a crisis of faith like God's love in action, as shown through his children.

+ Encourage the victim to take *everything* to God.

As a result of the pain and shock of the disaster, the victim may be struggling with some dark feelings and thoughts. The person may feel guilty about these thoughts. Help him or her understand that God is bigger than any problem we face, can handle our reactions, and already knows everything that is in the victim's heart and mind. Rather than feeling afraid or ashamed, remind the survivor that he or she can "come boldly to the throne of our gracious God" (Hebrews 4:16).

+ Surround the disaster survivor with caring community.

Scripture encourages us to connect with each other, to love one another, and to build healthy relationships. There are so many positive benefits of a healthy and caring community. By helping the disaster survivor connect to others through local church functions and small groups, you are doing the following:

• allowing God to use others to provide insight, help, and a listening ear to the survivor.

• helping the survivor navigate away from isolation and the depression that comes with it.

• opening resources to the survivor that may not have otherwise come to your mind.

• helping the person stay connected to his or her faith by connecting with loving, faithful people.

THE RIGHT QUESTION

A disaster brings out the obvious question: "Where was God?" This question and others like it are another form of the classic objection to Christianity: "Why would a good, loving, and all-powerful God allow evil?" Remember that the survivor of a disaster likely needs to be heard more than he or she needs to be lectured. But here are some thoughts on the question of why:

+ God values free will. God must value free will because he created a world where people have the real opportunity to choose evil or good. God isn't interested in relationship with robots or drones who must submit, obey, and love him. Rather, God wants people to choose relationship with him.

+ God has a different perspective. Since God is all-knowing and eternal, he has a different perspective on death than we do. In the light of eternity, our short time on earth and our transition through death is not as dramatic or traumatic as we view it.

+ God can bring good out of bad. If we look back on difficulties in our lives, it may be possible to see how God brought good out of bad situations. Each of us has experienced at least one difficult circumstance that we might not change even if we could because it has shaped who we have become.

We may never know *why* this disaster occurred. We all can gain insight and direction on the answerable question: *What* should I do now?

What Not to Say

+ "Don't say things like that."

A disaster survivor may make sarcastic or even frightening comments about faith and God. It may be difficult to hear such remarks because the person is talking about matters that are important to you. You may also fear that the person may be slipping away from Christ altogether.

More than anything, the survivor needs to work through the loss he or she has experienced. One important aspect of that work is talking about the shock and loss. The person needs to know that he or she can talk to you about what's really going on inside. By refraining from sharing your gut impulse of fear or anger, you'll become a person the survivor feels comfortable talking with.

+ "God causes everything to work together for the good of those who love him."

This statement is true. You can find it in Romans 8:28. However, you can't expect a victim of disaster to see the good in a disaster immediately after it has occurred. Think, for example, how you would feel if a well-intentioned person shared these words with you at the funeral of a loved one. Your reaction may be something like, "Are you saying God took my loved one for my own good?" People need time to work through grief and pain before they can start seeing the good that God can bring out of tragedy and disaster. There may come a time to share this Scripture, but it's likely not during the middle of a crisis of faith.

+ "You just have to move on."

When you ask someone to move on after a disaster, you may be asking the person to move on from some of the most precious memories and people of his or her life. Instead of telling the survivor of a disaster what he or she needs to do, ask the person what he or she needs *you* to do.

What to Say

✛ "I don't know why this happened."

When disaster strikes someone else, people sometimes try to find meaning in the disaster by attributing it to God's judgment. In Scripture we see that God clearly has brought disaster as a means of judgment. However, the account of Job, as well as Jesus' answer regarding the cause of a man's blindness in John 9, point to the fact that not all suffering is the result of judgment.

Admitting our ignorance will prevent us from making prideful interpretations that can cause someone in a faith crisis to move further from God.

✛ "How can I help you rebuild?"

This is the better alternative to "You just have to move on." By asking this question, you are making yourself available in areas where the survivor really needs and wants help. By using the word *rebuild,* you encourage the person to keep moving forward, but you are not requiring him or her to throw away all that came before the disaster. You can follow this up with another helpful question: "How can I pray for you?"

✛ "Your questions are a normal part of the process of dealing with disaster."

The disaster survivor needs to know that it's normal to go through serious reflection, doubt, and questioning after significant loss and pain. Challenge the person to try to walk through those difficulties in the context of Christian community and support rather than pushing current friends and support systems away. God is not afraid of questions and doubt. God's truth has stood the tests of time, suffering, and questioning. You, the survivor, and his or her support network should all work patiently through the struggles together and not be threatened or intimidated by questioning. And keep in mind that some questions just don't have earthly answers.

WHEN TO REFER

+ With the disaster survivor's permission, call upon his or her friends, pastor, leaders, and small group immediately. During a crisis of faith, the survivor needs support, love, and understanding from as many believers as possible. The person will likely isolate him- or herself to a degree. If friends fail to reach out in love, the person may easily misinterpret that as Christian hypocrisy or proof of their lack of real concern. You alone can't (and shouldn't) carry the survivor or be the only lifeline to truth and enduring faith. Call on the resources of the survivor's church group, or if that's not possible, on other local churches.

+ When you see signs of other problems. A crisis of faith could be a symptom of depression. Encourage the survivor to seek help from a professional counselor if you see signs of serious depression. (See Chapter 3.)

ADDITIONAL RESOURCES

+ Books

Lewis, C.S. *Mere Christianity.* New York: Macmillan Publishing, 1952.

Piper, John, and Justin Taylor. *Suffering and the Sovereignty of God*, Wheaton, IL: Crossway Books, 2006.

+ Online Resources

www.leadershipjournal.net (Real Ministry in a Complex World)

www.crosswalk.com (Crosswalk: The Intersection of Faith and Life)

CHAPTER TWO

Death and Bereavement
Helping Sufferers Through Loss

During the few weeks following the death of his wife, people had really reached out to Jim. They had brought food, had visited, and several women had offered to watch his children as he took care of the unexpected business of death. He had been numb; it was like being in a bad dream.

Unfortunately, he was starting to wake up. His grief was more intense now than in the first few weeks while he was in shock. However, now everyone was gone. No one stopped by; it seemed like people avoided him. Was he just becoming paranoid, or did people really act like they didn't see him? He knew that he had withdrawn from people because of the pain, but no one had followed.

He had disconnected from everyone and everything. Isolated and alone, he had lost perspective. It wasn't working; he was dying, too.

Jim slowly pulled into the driveway of the church. He had requested to meet with the pastor but was having second thoughts. Once an active member of the church, he had not entered the doors for six months. What would the pastor say to him? He sure wasn't in any mood for a lecture. The secretary who had scheduled the meeting was nice enough. She had asked if she could brief the pastor about the issue Jim wanted to meet with him about. There was a long pause as Jim's mind raced to find a way to answer what seemed to be a simple question.

It wasn't that there was no reason, but rather there were so many reasons that he didn't know where to start. This feeling of not knowing how to respond to life seemed to permeate his daily existence. Jim finally mumbled something about life being too overwhelming to deal with anymore.

How could he say that his wife had died suddenly in a car accident six months ago and he felt he had died with her? All that he had known was now gone, and he didn't really want to live any longer. But what about his three kids? They kept him alive, and yet he knew that they had to some degree lost their dad, too. They were dealing with their mother's death in a whole different way, and yet his grief was so overwhelming that he couldn't seem to find a way to help them through theirs.

Jim's friends always commented on how well he was doing and that they were so glad that he was OK. He hated that word. *OK.* What did that mean? On the outside, he breathed, got up every day, fixed meals, ate, went to work. To the outside world, he did everything that he did before. "OK?" No, he wasn't OK. Inside he was a mess. Perhaps the word that would best describe him was *lost.* Would he ever be found—were there any answers behind those church walls? Did God care? Did the church care? Could no one see the pain behind the outward appearance?

It seemed that no one could hear the silent screams that were tearing Jim apart. He didn't want to be "OK," and he didn't want anyone telling him that he would be OK. He wanted to rage, scream, yell at God. He was sick of the spiritual clichés that people were so quick to offer. Jim had walked with God for many years, and yet in his grief he felt alone, abandoned.

He did, however, take great comfort in reading the psalms. Psalm 23 had become a comfort for him, and yet he most resonated with the psalms of lament. He wondered why he never heard these psalms in church. These psalms were real cries, by real people. Void of the platitudes that he usually heard in church, the psalmists cried out from the depths of the soul. They felt forgotten, abandoned, rejected. They wondered if God had turned his face from them.

Sometimes Jim felt that the secondary wounds that he had experienced after the death of his wife were even more hurtful than her death. Were his expectations of God and the church too high? If he were a better Christian, would he be struggling less? Did everyone in the church have it together, or did they just put on a public face like he did? Where were all the wounded people like him? He desperately needed someone real, someone who had been beat up, someone who had walked through hell and come out on the other side still with God.

Jim stepped out of the car, measuring each step to the doors of the church. He desperately needed some answers. But more than anything else, he needed someone to walk with him in this unbearable, and what seemed to be unending, journey to healing. What would he find?

Care and Counseling Tips

THE BASICS

The aftermath of death and loss is a complex journey of recovery. While there are many common symptoms that survivors may experience following loss, it is a unique and individual journey through which survivors must travel. The church can play a powerful role in how survivors navigate this road and how they come out on the other side. Trauma and loss don't necessarily guarantee that a person will come out on the other side stronger, and yet there are many passages in the Bible that indicate that adverse circumstances can lead to significant personal growth and development.

Grief is all-encompassing and touches all aspects of a survivor's life. Too often, people only see the emotional impacts of grief. However, grief can have profound impacts on people from many dimensions, including physiologically, cognitively, emotionally, behaviorally, relationally, and spiritually.

Caregivers must be aware of the common reactions that survivors have to loss, but also understand the indicators of complicated grief and how to help survivors get help when needed.

Care Tips

+ Be present. One of the most powerful things that friends, family, and caregivers can do is to show up. However, you can be present in other ways such as a phone call or a handwritten note. Caregivers are often amazed at the appreciation that they receive from grieving individuals when acknowledged for just simply showing up.

+ Respect privacy. Your presence is ministry only if it is desired and comforting to the person. Sometimes, in the acute aftermath of loss, survivors may only want to be with their closest friends and family. Be sensitive and watch their nonverbal clues. Sometimes as a caregiver you may serve an immediate role to provide care until their closest family and friends show up. Know when to leave. You can always check in later.

+ Arrange continuing assistance. The church can play a critical role in linking survivors with long-term care so that they do not feel forgotten after the immediacy diminishes. Always remember that a person's critical need for others may be as strong as the months progress as during the immediate aftermath. Work with the survivor's church—or a nearby church—to arrange continuing assistance.

+ Share your story—with sensitivity. Often the most helpful people are those who have experienced similar experiences, have experienced healthy healing, and are able to give back to others. As long as these caregivers keep from telling too much of their own stories, they can help survivors walk where they have already been. They can bring hope to survivors that there is still life after major loss and understand from a perspective that others, including close friends, never can.

+ Provide practical care. Survivors almost always indicate that the practical things that people did for them in their times of loss and grief were the most helpful actions taken. Caregivers should try to identify the most critical needs and then link survivors with those who can best meet those needs. Too often well-meaning people say "call me if I can do anything." This rarely happens.

+ Make sure your actions are wanted. The best caregivers quickly assess what is needed—with the help and blessing of the survivor—and then take practical steps to meet those needs.

A word of caution: Sometimes well-intentioned caregivers can do harm if they take actions that aren't desired by the survivor. For example, when one woman's child died during labor, several family members and friends went to the home before she returned and removed all of the baby items from the nursery the parents had prepared.

The mother returned home, not only without the baby, but to an empty room devoid of all that she had lovingly prepared. These secondary wounds further exacerbated her loss.

Counseling Tips

✚ Maintain balance. Galatians 6:2-5 instructs us to "carry each other's burdens" but also that "each one should carry his own load" (NIV). There is a fine balance between doing *for* and doing *with*. In the aftermath of significant loss when a person is in a crisis state, that person often needs more help because his or her capacity to think and appropriately respond is diminished.

The degree of reaction is dependent on a person's personality. Some people will need to take an active role in regaining control of their situation, while others may be so overwhelmed by the situation that they are severely incapacitated. Help survivors find the balance between doing too much or too little. When in doubt, ask the survivor.

✚ Provide information. Information is power. Crisis responders often serve in a liaison or advocacy role to ensure that survivors get the critical information that they need. There are many unknowns that happen in times of loss, especially in a sudden and unexpected death. Survivors need information to begin putting their lives back together. Survivors also need to be prepared for what the road ahead of them will be like.

This is where support groups can help survivors because they are encouraged by others who have walked similar roads and can support them in their darkest hours. Survivors need to understand the common reactions that they may experience following loss and learn ways to cope with the way in which grief and loss can so pervasively change their lives. Prepare survivors to experience a wide range of emotions that will fluctuate over time.

✚ Make a plan. Helping survivors develop a care plan for the future is important. Too often, survivors are not prepared for the ways in which grief can take a toll on other relationships. Educating survivors how to take care of those still living, while continuing to take care of their own needs, is vital.

✚ Expect differences. Help families understand that each person will grieve loss differently. There are many unrecognized expectations we subconsciously place on grievers as to how to publicly mourn. Help survivors mourn their losses in a healthy way that is helpful to them, not necessarily in a way that is comfortable to you.

+ Expect shock and denial. In the immediate aftermath of loss, survivors may vacillate between denial and premature acceptance. Don't try to force people out of their state of shock. Shock and denial are important God-given coping mechanisms that allow people to absorb an unbelievable situation. However, using clear language in a loving way can begin to make the situation real. Use phrases such as "When John died," or "Since the cancer diagnosis."

+ Provide a safe place to talk. As time progresses, survivors may find that those closest to them weary of hearing them talk about their grief. It's common for survivors to hear, "You just need to move on." It's natural for us to want those we love to return to normal. But survivors know that they will never be "normal"; but they will, with time, develop a "new normal." Link survivors with local support groups. And it's especially important to link survivors to people who can be with them through the long haul. Romans 12:15 instructs us to "rejoice with those who rejoice; mourn with those who mourn" (NIV).

+ Defer to the survivor. If you're involved in helping the survivor plan a funeral or memorial service, ask what things would be most meaningful to the survivor, rather than assuming that what you usually do is relevant. Sometimes churches will make this mistake and create funerals that significantly miss the mark as to what would actually be helpful to the survivor.

+ Give the survivor permission to move on. Sometimes survivors feel disloyal to their loved ones when they begin to rebuild, and this can be a barrier to growth. Have an open discussion about this, and assure the survivor that it's natural and healthy to look forward.

+ Don't be afraid to talk about the deceased. Holidays and anniversaries can trigger strong emotions for survivors. Don't hesitate to talk about the deceased. Too often people are afraid to bring up the death for fear of making things worse. Talking about something funny you remember or something you shared together with the deceased can be meaningful to survivors.

+ **Help keep memories alive.** Survivors often discuss their fear of loved ones being forgotten. While some survivors find comfort in going to the graveside, others may not. Alternate ways of feeling a connection with the deceased might include such things as establishing a memorial fund, planting a tree, or placing a bench in a park with their loved one's name on it.

SCRIPTURE HELP

+ **Psalm 10:17; 13; 16; 18:8; 23; 31:9; 77; 119:25-32; 147:3**
+ **Ecclesiastes 3:4**
+ **Isaiah 41:10**
+ **Matthew 26:36-38**

+ **John 13:34-35**
+ **Romans 8:35-39; 12:15**
+ **2 Corinthians 1:3-7; 4:7-12; 6:3-10; 12:9**
+ **Philippians 1:6**
+ **James 1:2-4**

What Not to Say

+ "You can have another baby." Discounting statements like this minimize the survivor's pain and discount his or her feelings. Avoid statements that minimize the impact the loss has had on the survivor.

+ "It's God's will." Clichés, whether spiritual or secular, can be offensive even if they are true. People don't want your knowledge or religion until they have had your ear and heart of compassion!

+ "I know how you're feeling." Even if you, too, have suffered a recent loss, you can't *really* know the circumstances and emotions that the survivor has experienced. Your first goal should be to act as a sounding board for the survivor, so he or she can express thoughts and feelings.

What to Say

+ Speak nonverbally. Someone who can be a comforting, non-anxious presence in the midst of a person's pain is a rare gift. A touch on the arm, a hug, or a knowing smile speak volumes.

+ "I've wanted to pick up the phone so many times, but I didn't know what to say." Even if you don't know what to say, stay connected with the survivor. Admit that you may be at a loss for words or actions, but staying connected lets the survivor know that you care.

+ "How can I help you through this time?" This statement shows that you care, and it also opens the door for the survivor to talk. Survivors feel isolated in their loss, and while they sometimes need time alone, they desperately want to be connected to healthy people who love and care for them.

+ "I really miss [name of deceased]." Let the survivor know that you haven't forgotten the deceased, and that you miss him or her.

+ "What is the hardest thing for you right now?" Caring questions can convey concern and allow a safe space for survivors to talk. Take time from your schedule to ask caring questions—and then *listen* to the responses!

WHEN TO REFER

+ When you can't do it all. It's critical for a caregiver to understand the limits of his or her capacity to help another person. Sometimes we are slow to refer because we think we can do it all. It's necessary for the caregiver to distinguish between what is needed to stabilize a person on scene and what is needed for the long-term recovery journey.

+ When the survivor demonstrates an unusually high death anxiety about self or loved ones. Sometimes a survivor will develop oversensitivity and/or overreaction to experiences entailing loss and separation. This fear will inhibit healing and needs to be addressed.

+ When you sense a chronic sense of numbing, alienation, or depersonalization. Isolating behavior serves as a buffer at first, but when it extends beyond the initial shock, it's time to evaluate the survivor's well-being. Withdrawal from close relationships and an inability to form new relationships for fear of loss can lead to a pattern of self-destructive relationships.

+ When you observe marked behavioral change. Behavioral changes may include restlessness, incessant activity, rigidity, depression, inability to talk about the death, and compulsive or ritualistic behavior. You may also notice substance dependence or abuse.

+ When you notice a pattern of self-destructive relationships. Sometimes survivors begin or escalate unhealthy relationships subsequent to the loss. These relationships may include compulsive care-giving and replacement relationships.

+ When the survivor experiences a crisis of faith. Left unattended, this secondary crisis and loss can seriously impact the survivor's life.

CHAPTER THREE

Depression
When the Darkness Outlasts the Storm

Before reaching Louisiana and Texas, Hurricane Rita was the fourth strongest hurricane ever recorded. It caused more than $11 billion dollars in damage after it made landfall. Even though the storm surged to 15 to 20 feet on the coast near Emily's home of Lake Charles, the flooding and initial winds didn't damage her home. However, tornadoes ripped through Louisiana in the storm's wake. One of those tornadoes destroyed Emily's barn, killed some of her livestock, and damaged her home.

But Emily's real trial began after the storm. Emily recalls looking over her neighborhood at a sea of blue roofs covered with tarps in a feeble effort to keep out further weather damage and insects. Fallen trees and overturned cars blocked the roads. The city came to a standstill as power was lost and travel was nearly impossible. Most of Lake Charles was without running water and electricity for days. Generators were available, but fuel for the generators was nearly impossible to find. Homes started to rot from the mildew and moisture, and the standing water became the breeding ground for a tempest of mosquitoes.

The National Guard set up a camp in front of a Wal-Mart and distributed emergency rations. "At first, we all grumbled and complained about the lousy food," Emily remembers. "But when everything in our freezers and refrigerators started to rot, we were happy to have it."

The first tears came as Emily and her husband "celebrated" their 47th wedding anniversary over military rations. Emily was surprised how often and easily she would find herself in tears months and even years after the storm. She cries today as she tells the story of how her neighbors finally returned four weeks after the storm to find their dog starved to death inside of the home. "I could have saved the dog if I had just known it was in there," laments Emily. She describes carrying a burden of anxiety and heaviness wherever she went. Discovering the decimation of favorite stores, landmarks, and churches, only added a dark weight to Emily's heavy heart.

The greatest loss for Emily came when she lost her friend and neighbor, Theodore. Just prior to the storm, Theo had gone through a difficult divorce. When the tornado took his home, car, and boat, Theo felt like he had nothing left to live for. He ended his own life by overdosing on prescription medication.

"My depression started to subside when I started to see progress," Emily remarks. The slow process of rebuilding was the healing balm to Emily's burdened and depressed heart. Streets slowly cleared and people began to go back to work. Fast-food restaurants offered starting bonuses since so many people had left the area for good. "The Salvation Army was a gift from God," remembers Emily. "It seems like those people were the only ones who really did any good. They were everywhere with blankets and clothes."

Even though Emily started to feel better, she remembers one day in particular when she finally felt truly free from the weight of the storm. "On the day we finally decided to leave Lake Charles, I felt like a weight was lifted off my back. My son still lives there, and he's sticking it out. But I just couldn't go through another hurricane season."

Three years after hurricane Rita, Emily and her husband moved to Colorado. "Every place has its natural disasters, but I don't think any hurricanes will reach us there," Emily jokes.

Care and Counseling Tips

THE BASICS

The effects of disasters remain long after emergency aid has come and gone. A disaster brings loss to its victims, and depression is a very common response to loss. Disaster victims may struggle through the obvious loss of friends or family, loss of property and the memories associated with it, or the loss of certain infrastructures. Nearly all disaster victims struggle with a loss of their sense of security and find it difficult, if not impossible, to go back to life as it was.

Depression is a normal and common response to the loss a person experiences during a disaster. In fact, depression is one of the stages typically associated with grief and loss. Depression is a dark and oppressive mood problem that can feel unbearable to the person suffering from it. The burden of depression drags the person down as he or she tries to carry on with life as usual when life is not "as usual."

Yet there is hope. By understanding the basic symptoms and causes of depression and learning to express care in ways that will be received well by the person who is depressed, you can share the burden of depression with a disaster survivor, and he or she will begin to feel the weight of depression lift. Look for the following symptoms of depression after a disaster:

+ Emotional Symptoms of Depression

A depressed mood is usually characterized by hopelessness, sadness, discouragement, anxiety, and/or irritability all day, nearly every day for two weeks. These internal feelings may manifest in behaviors such as frequent crying, sharp and hurtful comments, a pessimistic outlook, and statements that reveal a sense of being overwhelmed by life. Many depressed people report a loss of interest or participation in activities that they previously found enjoyable.

+ Physical Symptoms of Depression

The body has a way of manifesting symptoms when a person is suffering emotionally. Depressed people may experience a change in appetite and in sleep patterns. In addition, depressed people tend to have several physical complaints and often make more trips to the doctor than usual.

+ Cognitive Symptoms of Depression

People who experience depression as a result of a disaster may struggle with excessive guilt. While it is normal to wonder why others may have encountered a more horrible fate, take notice if the victim shows a strong and recurring sense of guilt for surviving. Moreover, people struggling with depression may have difficulty thinking clearly, concentrating, or making decisions. If untreated, depression can lead to thoughts of death or, in the worst case, suicide. Be sensitive to comments such as, "I just want to fall asleep forever," or "I can't go on like this anymore."

+ Behavioral Symptoms of Depression

Decreased energy, tiredness, and fatigue are characteristics of depression. You may notice that the victim's house has not been cleaned in some time, personal hygiene has declined, or he or she is sleeping much more than usual or isolating him- or herself from friends and other important relationships.

+ Spiritual Symptoms of Depression

When a person is depressed, he or she may have a hard time connecting with God and believing in God's goodness and providence. Prayer may become difficult, as the person may feel hopeless or guilty for not praying enough, in the right way, or about the right things. If the person's individual spirituality suffers during depression, corporate spirituality is likely to suffer as well. That is, he or she may have difficulty getting to church due to fatigue, and once at church, worship may be difficult. It is not unusual for a person who has endured a disaster to struggle through a crisis of faith.

Care Tips

When a person is experiencing depression, it's difficult to know how to be present in the darkness. You want to let the disaster survivor know that you are caring and supportive, but you may feel drained by the heaviness and pessimism when you are with him or her. Here are some tips to help you serve the person during the struggle to get out of depression:

+ Actively listen.

Encouraging the survivor to talk about his or her sadness will foster understanding, which can help foster a sense of control over emotions instead of feeling controlled by emotions. Although the feelings may frighten you, don't be afraid; just listen as you would to any friend of yours.

+ Spend time with the disaster survivor.

When a person is depressed, the natural tendency is to hide from others and try to recover on one's own. The survivor may be hiding because he or she is afraid of appearing weak or disturbed. Or the person may have reasoned that others couldn't possibly understand what he or she has gone through. But that's exactly the opposite of what is needed. A depressed person needs other people! Your presence will help shoulder the burden of depression, allow for rest, stave off loneliness, guard against suicide, and provide strength. Don't pretend to completely understand what the person is going through. Rather, clearly demonstrate your desire to remain available and ready to listen through this life-changing event.

+ Suggest enjoyable activities.

The disaster victim may not be able to come up with enjoyable activities due to a lack of excitement and joy. Suggest activities that he or she once enjoyed or those that you enjoy. Even if the person seems resistant, there is likely a part of him or her that longs to do enjoyable things—it's simply buried under depression. Be persistent—human contact and enjoyable activities are essential for acceptance and healing. A light-hearted diversion will help the person understand that there is life beyond the disaster he or she has experienced.

+ Exercise.

It's a vicious cycle. The fatigue and lack of motivation caused by depression significantly impairs a depressed person's ability to exercise…but regular exercise has been shown to be a buffer against depression. You will be helping the survivor immensely by encouraging him or her to exercise regularly. It can be anything the person desires: playing a sport, taking an exercise class, or taking a walk around the neighborhood. The person simply needs to get out and get moving.

+ Be nonjudgmental.

Depressed people judge themselves every day, so the last thing they need is a friend who judges them, too. Communicate patience and grace. By doing this, you may help the victim become more patient and gracious toward him- or herself. Point out the positive steps he or she has made, and encourage him or her toward the future.

Counseling Tips

Many times depression calls for a professional counselor. Even so, there are many ways you can personally help coach the disaster survivor through this tough time:

+ Build and maintain trust.

Trust takes time—it takes positive experiences built on more positive experiences. But once trust is built, it's easy to break—especially when things said in secret are later shared with others. As you comfort and connect with the survivor, be sure to keep a policy of confidentiality—the *only* time you should talk to someone else is if the person is endangering him- or herself or another person, or if you have asked permission to share information.

+ Validate and normalize emotions.

Without crawling into the pit of depression with the victim, you can validate his or her emotions by expressing understanding and care. Normalizing depression can also help the person feel less alone in the process. It is damaging and counterproductive to point out that others suffered greater loss in the event. But helping the person understand that depression is a very common and valid response to such situations will help validate that the difficult emotions he or she is experiencing won't last with such recurring intensity forever.

+ Challenge faulty thinking.

Depression impairs people's thinking. Depressed people often feel unworthy of good relationships, success at their jobs, or a peaceful lifestyle. They often think that God has cursed them and that life is hopeless. If the disaster survivor expresses these feelings, speak the truth of God's love. Remind the person that recovery from depression is a process, but it's treatable through professional counseling, fellowship, prayer, time, and medication, if necessary.

+ Create positive affirmations and experiences.

Depression clouds the ability to think positively. One way to counter this is to help the disaster victim come up with positive truths. Consider suggesting or going through a Bible study together that focuses on what God says about his children, or start a small group that focuses on dealing with loss or grief. Consider joining the victim in reaching out to and helping other victims of the disaster in clean up or other service efforts.

It is likely that the person may experience overwhelming emotion when encountering the disaster again. Don't push him or her to go faster or deeper than he or she is ready to go. But working through these emotions can actually help the victim work through depression.

+ Trust God for the disaster victim.

Don't be afraid to make mistakes. Trust God as you learn to care for and counsel the victim of disaster. Pray for the person regularly, and ask God to give you wisdom and insight into the victim's heart.

Ministry Tips

+ Invite the disaster survivor to be part of a group.

There are few thing as powerful as caring community and relationships when a person is struggling with loss and depression. If you're already part of a small group or Bible study, invite the victim in. If he or she doesn't feel ready for the intimacy of a home group, invite him or her to church with you. Provide opportunities for the person to connect with others at church through low-risk events such as potlucks, game nights, or service project events.

+ Look to God.

Don't feel the burden to "fix" the survivor of a disaster, because you can't. But God can make things right in the person's mind, heart, and emotions. The most effective and powerful ministry often comes through earnest listening and heartfelt prayer. Pray regularly for and with the survivor. If you don't have the answer to a question or dilemma, pray together. And encourage the person to look to God first for help.

+ Share your struggles with the survivor.

Scripture tells us in Galatians 6:2 to share each other's burdens. The person you are helping shouldn't feel like he or she is your project. Rather, you should develop a relationship together that points each other to Jesus. While you may do the majority of the "carrying" at this time, let the survivor into your life so he or she can see that you are engaged in a two-way friendship. Your transparency will help you both experience the joy of fulfilling God's command in Galatians 6:2.

What Not to Say

+ "As Christians, we should show the joy of the Lord."

This statement leaves no room for the spectrum of emotions common to the human experience. By making statements like this, you'll only cause the victim to feel further away from God than he or she already does. The person is probably aware that depression is not God's emotional design for anyone but still can't just stop being depressed. As Christians, we should be human and show support and love when others are struggling to find joy.

+ "Stop being so negative, and look at the positive."

This statement may be said with good intentions, but looking at the good things in life isn't the answer for a person with serious depression. While negative thought patterns are one aspect of depression, it's a more complicated matter—depression isn't a choice and can't just disappear with an attitude adjustment. If the disaster survivor could simply "not be so negative," he or she would. Saying something of this nature would be like telling a blind person to not be so blind.

+ "I know that you're better than this—don't give in!"

Saying this suggests that the victim is falling short and somehow failing to control emotions. The person is likely already dealing with issues of self-worth and feelings of failure—this statement will only confirm those feelings.

What to Say

+ "This probably isn't the best time to make a decision like this."
In an effort to avoid or shake negative emotions, a person who is struggling with depression as a result of a disaster may try to make a radical change. Filing for divorce, seeking to move, quitting a job, or changing churches may look like the only way out to the survivor. Encourage the person to avoid life-altering decisions until he or she has had some time to process what is going on inside.

+ "God is with you in this dark time."
By telling the survivor this, you're reminding him or her of the relentless presence of God in all emotional states. You're telling the person that God is no stranger to depression and that he won't leave or disappear when life is tough.

+ "How can I pray for you?"
With this statement, you're communicating that you wish to accommodate the victim spiritually as he or she journeys through this darkness.

+ "If you ever need anything, I'm here. I'll call you on Friday to see how you're doing."
Someone struggling with depression has a hard time taking a first step with friends and needs to be pursued. Letting someone know you'll be there can be powerful. Be sincere, and then follow through on your words.

+ "I've been thinking about you today."
This statement reveals that you care. Follow it with thoughtful questions. Anything that shows you listened to a previous conversation and remembered what the survivor said will demonstrate that you believe he or she is worth listening to and paying attention to.

+ "You're doing a great job with..."

Confirm that the person with depression is worthwhile, despite what he or she may be feeling. Focus on positives even if he or she is incapable of doing so.

WHEN TO REFER

+ When a disaster survivor becomes suicidal.

If the survivor expresses a desire to end his or her life, get help.

+ When a disaster survivor is a danger to others.

If the survivor expresses a sincere desire to harm another person, refer him or her to a mental health care worker, and notify the person whom he or she plans to harm.

+ When a child is endangered or neglected.

If the survivor has children or works with children and is unable to care for them, encourage the person to get help. Help the survivor to seek family members or friends who can take the children for a time, or notify child protective services, if necessary.

+ When a survivor's daily functioning is impaired.

Depression can impair a person's social, occupational, and personal functioning. If you know that he or she is not engaging socially, his or her work performance is suffering, or the survivor is unable to get out of bed, feed, groom, and/or bathe, get help.

SCRIPTURE HELP

+ **Psalm 31; 32:1-7**
+ **Psalm 42:1-5**
+ **Psalm 139**
+ **Isaiah 40:29-31**
+ **Jeremiah 17:5-8**

+ **Romans 15:13**
+ **2 Corinthians 1:3-11**
+ **2 Corinthians 4:8-9**
+ **Ephesians 6:10-18**
+ **Philippians 4:4-8**

ADDITIONAL RESOURCES

+ Books

Daniels, Linda. *Healing Journeys: How Trauma Survivors Learn to Live Again.* Far Hills, NJ: New Horizon Press, 2004.

Tan, Siang-Yang, and John Ortberg. *Coping with Depression.* Grand Rapids, MI: Baker Books, 2004.

Worthington, Everett L. *When Someone Asks for Help: A Practical Guide for Counseling.* Downers Grove, IL: InterVarsity Press, 1982.

+ Online Resources

www.nimh.nih.gov/publicat/friend.cfm (National Institute of Mental Health)

www.healthyminds.org (American Psychiatric Association)

www.suicidology.org (American Association of Suicidology)

www.dbsalliance.org (Depression and Bipolar Support Alliance)

CHAPTER FOUR

Suicide
Intervening Before It's Too Late

I met Martha at the middle of a long bridge. She sat on a bright red Radio Flyer wagon. I had watched her from the mainland shore for about 30 minutes before I ventured out on the bridge to talk to her. As I approached her there at the high point of the bridge, she looked up from the wagon and spoke before I could even introduce myself.

"Is there anything left to live for?" she asked. Immediately I felt the angst of the moment, for her and for me. How was I going to answer this woman's question? Did I even have an answer?

I had exchanged passing comments with Martha about two hours earlier on the approach to the bridge. She was there as a victim of Hurricane Ivan, and I was there as a Salvation Army Disaster Officer. I was providing water and snacks to the 200 or so residents of Navarre Beach, Florida. Navarre is actually an island and is only connected to the mainland by this one bridge. Officials had just opened the bridge to foot traffic solely for residents of the island.

Martha was a retired lawyer around 72 years young. She and her husband had retired six years earlier and had purchased a condo right on the beach in Navarre. All of what they considered valuable in their life was centered in that condo. Mementos of great occasions and family triumphs, pictures of children and grandchildren. This was their haven, the result of a life of toil and saving so they could enjoy the "great life" on the beach in their sunset years.

With reluctance, the two of them had evacuated the condo before the arrival of Ivan. Just before the storm, they had driven all the way to Memphis to stay with their daughter. The hasty and long trip through the night proved to be too much for Martha's husband. The next morning as Ivan crashed into the Florida coast, he died of a massive heart attack.

It was more than a week since Ivan had struck, and now for the first time the residents were allowed back on the island to visit their homes. They were only permitted to walk across the damaged bridge with small baskets or carts to bring back a few important items. With a broken heart, Martha had ventured across less than two hours earlier with the wagon, in hopes of bringing back some precious reminders of the life she had treasured with her beloved husband. On her return from the condo, she had stopped in the middle of the bridge. That's where I encountered her, staring at the now-placid waters of the inlet. That's where she asked, "Is there anything left to live for?"

In a rush, all the crisis counseling methods and phrases I had studied ran through my mind. But nothing seemed appropriate for the moment. Martha continued to pour out her anxiety. She had gone back to the condo only to discover that the seaside window that had been such a pleasure was gone. The entire unit was filled with sand and debris. There was nothing left to salvage.

Her entire life was represented by an empty wagon in the middle of a shaky bridge. All I could do was to let her talk. Soon I began to respond to the details of her story. "Where are your children? Do you have grandchildren? What will you do now?"

As she talked, she discovered for herself the answer to her main question. There was a great deal left to live for, and as I walked beside her back to her car on the mainland, she began on her own to point out the real foundations of her life. All of the "things" of life were only things. The essence of who we are is within. Her spiritual foundations were slowly emerging as the door of tacit permission was open for me to remind her that even in the hour of greatest despair, God still loves us and ultimately has a plan for our lives. I didn't preach a sermon—only those brief words.

"Yes," she said. "I know, but I needed you to remind me. I really did think of jumping back there on the bridge, but my heart kept telling me to wait—wait. And then you came."

The key element in counseling after a disaster, even for someone distressed to the point of contemplating suicide, is first to listen, and for me, then to pray and to "be there" as the struggle unfolds.

Before Martha left, I made a call to Memphis and was able to put her in contact with a qualified Christian counselor.

Are there considerations of suicide after disaster? Yes. Many times, I am sure. Be prepared in heart, mind, and spirit to share those moments, to help bear the pain, and to give counsel to the best of your ability.

Care and Counseling Tips

THE BASICS

Ultimately, your job is simple. If you suspect the person you're working with is considering suicide, it's your role to persuade the person to get professional help. However, reality is often more complex. The first thing to do is learn to detect the presence of suicidal thoughts. Many people will directly tell you that they're thinking about suicide. For others, you'll have to know the warning signs, which fall into two categories: what the person says and what the person does.

+ What the Person Says

In the aftermath of a disaster, the range of emotions you may encounter can be spread over the entire spectrum. People experiencing emotional pain that may lead to suicide sometimes communicate it verbally, although perhaps in a disguised way. Types of verbal warnings may include any of the following:

1. Any comment that implies life isn't worth the effort. For instance, "Life's too painful; I don't think I want to deal with it anymore."

2. Any comment that shows the person believes there's no solution to his or her problems. For example, "There's no way out of this mess."

3. Any statement implying that others "would be better off" if the person wasn't around.

4. An offer to give up some essential possessions because they'll no longer be needed. For example, "You can have some of my clothes; I don't think I'll be needing them."

5. Any indication that the person may take revenge by hurting him- or herself. For instance, "They'll wish they had done more when I'm gone."

+ What the Person Does

Sometimes a suicide attempt is impulsive, but other times the person may develop plans for an attempt. The person may begin to make financial arrangements for family, give away personal items or more money than usual, or plan a suicide note. People may also begin to engage in reckless and dangerous activities, such as increasing alcohol and drug use. Other signs include dramatic mood changes, intense anxiety, or signs of depression. Most importantly, if the person has begun to develop a plan (if he or she has bought a weapon, stored up pills, or thought about a specific scenario such as jumping off a nearby bridge), he or she is at *high* risk for suicide.

—*Some information in this section is adapted from www.stopasuicide.org.*

SCRIPTURE HELP

+ **Psalm 25:4-7, 15-21**
+ **Isaiah 40:27-31**
+ **Isaiah 41:9-10**
+ **Matthew 10:29-31**
+ **Matthew 11:28-30**
+ **Romans 8:35-39**
+ **2 Corinthians 1:3-11**
+ **2 Corinthians 12:7-10**
+ **Philippians 1:19-26**
+ **1 Peter 5:6-10**

Care Tips

If the disaster survivor has told you directly that he or she is considering suicide or you have detected one or more of the warning signs, it is *essential* that you ACT quickly and lovingly. (ACT is a useful acronym for remembering your responsibilities. See www.stopasuicide.org for more information.) The following are guidelines for your immediate response.

+ Acknowledge the problem.

Take it seriously—Never doubt that the survivor is actually considering suicide.

Listen without judgment or criticism—This will increase your credibility when you suggest professional help, and it may increase the survivor's willingness to agree.

+ Care for your friend.

Voice your concern—Ask the survivor what specifically is troubling him or her. Be gentle, and try to overcome reluctance to open up about private and painful thoughts.

Express care and understanding—Assure the survivor that he or she will be supported in this crisis. Assure the person that, though a real feeling, it's also temporary and that the usual cause of suicidal thoughts, depression, can be treated.

Find out if there is a specific plan—How detailed is the plan? Has he or she taken any steps toward implementing the plan? Has a time and a place been set? Encourage the survivor to talk about his or her plans, and determine the seriousness of the threat.

+ Treatment—always get help immediately.

If the survivor is willing to accept help—Take him or her to the local emergency room or mental health center. You can also contact the survivor's primary care physician or a mental health provider. Whomever you choose to contact, stay with the survivor, and accompany him or her to the professional service provider.

If the survivor is unwilling to seek help—Call the national help line or your local emergency room for assistance (see the "When to Refer" box on this page).

WHEN TO REFER

+ Always!—It's always possible that you've overestimated the person's risk of suicide. However, in this situation, it's better to err on the safe side. You'll rest easier knowing that you've done the best thing possible for the person.

+ Always!—If the risk for suicide seems to be high, there are several things you can do. First, the disaster survivor could call the National Suicide Prevention Lifeline (1-800-273-TALK). Second, if the person is unwilling to talk about his or her feelings and plans, you can call 911 for an emergency response team. Finally, you may be of greatest service by driving the person to the nearest emergency room for evaluation.

+ Always!—Even if the disaster survivor appears to be at low risk for suicide, you should insist on joining him or her in the process of seeking professional intervention. Professionals include psychologists and counselors, suicide prevention centers, a family doctor, or a minister. Go with the hurting person to the professional.

Counseling Tips

Ideally, you have helped the disaster survivor identify and engage in professional help. Now your job is to support the professional services the survivor is receiving and help achieve his or her therapeutic goals. Your contributions may include any of the following:

+ Openly communicate about the survivor's suicidal feelings.

Meet the person's need to talk about these feelings with someone besides a counselor. Help develop a sense that others care and want to openly discuss his or her difficulties.

+ Relieve isolation.

Isolation can intensify suicidal thoughts and depression. Suggest social support and activities. However, be sensitive to individual preferences in activities, and do not be overbearing. At the same time, don't allow the survivor to withdraw from social life and caring friends. Try to help the survivor re-establish social patterns while communicating your willingness to be available more frequently if desired.

+ Remove lethal weapons.

One of the first therapeutic goals of the professional counselor will be to remove all lethal weapons (including things such as pills, guns, knives, and so on) from the person's possession in order to protect the person from impulsively attempting suicide. Make yourself available to help complete this task. If possible, ask the survivor for the name of a close friend who can hold the survivor accountable for keeping lethal objects out of the home. Each individual will require different levels of accountability. For some individuals, a daily or weekly phone call may be enough. For others, it may be necessary to inspect the home frequently. Try to gauge the honesty of the survivor's self-report, and if you have some doubt about his or her safety, ask gently if you or the friend the survivor has chosen might be able to more closely monitor the home and behaviors.

+ Be a safe receptacle of the disaster survivor's anger and frustration.

Oftentimes, suicide is preceded by a sense that there is no escape from emotional pain. If you feel up to the challenge, allow the survivor to express his or her anger and frustration to you. Help the person understand the importance of doing so, rather than turning those feelings inward and hurting him- or herself.

+ Don't offer glib reassurance. Acknowledge the difficulty of the feelings and the need for help.

It can be demoralizing for someone who's considering suicide to be offered glib reassurance. Likely, your friend will have already tried many coping strategies and may have arrived at the conclusion that recovery is going to be difficult and painful—if not impossible. Try not to invalidate those feelings by minimizing the magnitude of the problem.

+ Pray.

In the person's current emotional state, he or she may have difficulty perceiving God as loving and benevolent. You may need to model God's love for the survivor until he or she is able to connect with God again.

What Not to Say

+ "I dare you to do it."

Don't laugh—this happens, and people who say it are usually well-intentioned. People think that they'll call the person's bluff by essentially telling him or her to do it. This is a *bad* idea. In the person's hopeless state of mind, it may be further evidence that he or she isn't valued.

+ "Ohmigosh, I can't believe you would even think that!"

Don't act surprised at the mention of suicide. This response may further the person's sense of shame and guilt, and it won't allow the survivor to trust you and your desire to help. The person's problem is very real and very serious—try not to invalidate it.

+ "Sure, I promise not to tell anyone."

Don't let yourself be sworn to secrecy. Also, don't worry if you have already agreed to secrecy. Let the survivor know why you won't be able to keep the agreement—he or she may initially be upset but will thank you in the long run. Feel confident that it's in the person's best interest to speak with others.

+ "Suicide is a sin."

The last thing the hurting person needs is an intellectual or theological debate. Instead, the person is probably craving someone who can be there for him or her emotionally. You can be far more helpful if you work hard to empathize with the survivor and convince him or her to seek professional help.

+ "Where is your faith? Things will get better."

It *is* important to tell the hurting person that the suicidal feelings are not permanent and that his or her ability to consider alternative solutions will return. However, it's also important to do so *without* questioning the person's faith. As you offer care during this difficult time, you'll naturally have opportunities to talk about faith. But to question the survivor's faith at the outset will likely put distance between the two of you and decrease your ability to help.

IMPORTANT FACTS

ABOUT SUICIDE

✚ Suicide is the 11th leading cause of death among all Americans.

✚ The suicide rate is highest among individuals over the age of 65.

✚ Although three times as many women attempt suicide compared to men, four times as many men are successful as compared to women.

✚ Guns are the most common method of suicide.

✚ Surviving family members may be at higher risk of also committing suicide.

✚ Youth (ages 15 to 24) suicide rates increased more than 200% from the 1950s to the late 1970s and have remained stable since then.

Facts taken from the American Association of Suicidology (www.suicidology.org).

What to Say

+ "Are you thinking about committing suicide?"

Many people hesitate to ask this question due to concern that it will offend the person or will plant the idea in his or her mind. Don't worry about that! With this question, you're more likely to communicate genuine concern than to make someone angry or offended. Furthermore, it's unlikely someone who isn't considering suicide will begin to do so simply because you asked a question.

+ "Let *others* be hopeful for you until you're ready to be hopeful again."

This implies several important things. First, it communicates that support is available to the survivor. Second, it says that you understand how hopeless the disaster survivor feels right now. Third, it communicates that you're confident the person will emerge from this situation and become hopeful again.

+ "I know this is an issue that doesn't get talked about enough. When you feel ready, would you be willing to work with me to start a support group for other survivors who are feeling depressed and suicidal?"

It's important to communicate that the survivor is not alone. By saying this, you imply that others need to be supportively discussing the topic more often in the aftermath of a disaster. And offering hope that the person could contribute to helping others is likely to increase his or her sense of self-worth.

+ "I love you, and as your friend in Christ, I won't abandon you at this time. What can I do to help?"

This is a key message to communicate to the hurting person. The disaster survivor may be feeling as if no one cares or no one cares enough to reach out. This will dispel that false belief. You also don't impose upon the person your own ideas about what might be helpful, but you allow the person's unique needs to guide you. An important thing to remember: If you make this offer, be sure you're ready to back it up. Honestly evaluate and communicate the amount of time and effort you'll be able to provide, and have a list of local resources available to the survivor.

ADDITIONAL RESOURCES

+ Books

Fine, Carla. *No Time to Say Goodbye: Surviving the Suicide of a Loved One.* New York, NY: Broadway Books, 1999.

+ Online Resources

www.stopasuicide.org (Screening for Mental Health, Inc.)

www.suicidology.org (American Association of Suicidology)

www.afsp.org (American Foundation for Suicide Prevention)

www.spanusa.org (Suicide Prevention Action Network USA)

CHAPTER **FIVE**

Financial Crisis
Overcoming the Insecurities
of Money Trouble

The flash flood warning on the news didn't really concern Dalton. Serious floods weren't that common in northern Colorado, and they were usually connected with channeled canyons or rivers. The Poudre River ran miles to the north of his trailer, and he was nowhere near a canyon. Dalton remained at home watching television over the sound of heavy rains coming down on his home.

But the Spring Creek Flood was anything but normal. On July 27th, a storm system saturated the ground of Fort Collins with 4 to 6 inches of rain. The next night, a second round of storms dumped 10 inches of rain in less than five hours. The tiny Spring Creek swelled over its banks. A stretch of railroad tracks served as an unintended levee, gathering the water. As the "levee" was breached, the little creek became a torrent that derailed a train and destroyed two mobile home parks.

Dalton heard a noise outside, which he imagined to be a broken power line. He was amazed to find knee-deep water rushing through his yard. He stopped just in time to notice that the steps from his trailer were floating away. As the sound of rushing water grew louder, Dalton scrambled to get to safety. He helped his wife climb up into a tree and then climbed to the roof. Dalton and his wife watched in terror as other trailers crumbled from the force of the flood and cars floated under the tree where his wife clung to life.

Rescue workers were forced to brave hot power lines that had been downed by the storm. The image of burning trailers above the lakelike mobile home park provided a surreal backdrop to the rescue. Late that night, a motorized raft slowly approached Dalton. Five people died in the disaster, but Dalton and his wife were taken to safety.

When Dalton was finally allowed to return to his home, he found that *everything* was gone from his trailer. All his appliances and furniture had either floated away or been looted. And they were never found again. Dalton was faced with the overwhelming task of starting all over again.

Dalton had spent the last number of decades scraping by to make ends meet. Starting over was almost too much for him and his wife to bear. He hadn't seen the sense in carrying insurance on his trailer or belongings, as he never imagined a disaster like the Spring Creek Flood would ever threaten his home.

Aid groups brought in food and clothing vouchers after the disaster, and Dalton was amazed that he never went hungry despite having an empty wallet and a missing refrigerator. Nearly every government representative encouraged Dalton not to panic. They reminded Dalton how easy it was to get confused and make poor decisions that outlasted the effects of the disaster.

Within a few days of the flood, FEMA distributed vouchers for apartments for rent. Dalton secured a voucher and moved into his new home. With the basic needs of food and shelter met, Dalton was able to slowly dig his way out of his financial crisis. He was met with a variety of responses—some of his creditors forgave debts, while others demanded that he pay for items that had floated to parts unknown.

At first, Dalton was nearly paralyzed by hopelessness and sadness. But as he moved into the home provided by FEMA, he began to feel a sense of hope. Dalton and his wife had to watch every penny, and they had to pass up even the most basic luxuries. Despite the crises, thankfulness permeated his new environment. Memories of his wife clinging to a tree made Dalton happy that both of them were still alive.

Dalton still hasn't replaced all the comforts of his old home, and he will never retrieve the photographs and small heirlooms that were washed away. But Dalton is living within his means, enjoying life in his apartment, and slowly moving forward financially.

SCRIPTURE HELP

+ **Deuteronomy 8:2-5, 17-18**
+ **Psalm 62:5-10**
+ **Proverbs 3:5-10**
+ **Proverbs 30:8-9**
+ **Jeremiah 9:23-24**
+ **Luke 6:20-21**
+ **Luke 12:15-21**
+ **Philippians 4:6-7, 11-13**
+ **1 Timothy 6:6-10, 17-19**
+ **James 1:2-12**

Care and Counseling Tips

THE BASICS

Helping a person in financial crisis due to a disaster can be a daunting task. A disaster often hits people hardest who are poor or in lower income brackets. Lower-income families often can't afford adequate home and health insurance to cope with a disaster. There is less likelihood that a poor family has strong support structures. And low-income families sometimes are forced to choose housing options that are less resistant to disasters or are located in higher-risk areas.

The financial need may be so great that you may feel that you can't make a real difference. There are two essential truths to hold onto when these feelings of discouragement come:

1. A small amount of help is exponentially better than no help at all. The survivor of a disaster has a long road to travel. Your assistance may not solve the problem, but it will most certainly help him or her keep going toward the solution. If we had to solve a problem to make working on it worthwhile, there would be no point in most social support programs.

2. The help you provide is as much or even more about the spiritual and emotional health of a disaster survivor as it is about the financial and physical needs he or she has. A financial crisis is frightening and overwhelming, it forces big changes in a person's life, and it takes time to make it through. More than anything, the survivor needs hope for the future. Your involvement can provide the hope that empowers the person to keep striving for financial freedom. While creditors can be intimidating, the survivor's greatest threats come from discouragement, hopelessness, and depression.

Care Tips

More than many other problems, financial crises have a way of threatening our basic sense of security. Your goal in the initial stage of caring for a survivor is to protect him or her against the fear associated with financial insecurity. The following steps are most effective if implemented sequentially, and ideally they should be accomplished as quickly as possible.

+ Assess the situation and identify sustaining factors.

Don't hesitate to engage the person in a discussion about his or her financial problems. Most people will be eager to accept help in a financial crisis. However, be aware of the possibility that the person may not initially want to discuss the problem in great depth. Help him or her investigate available solutions and support for the dilemma. What assistance can the disaster victim find through insurance, disaster recovery programs, federal or local programs, or charitable organizations? Help the survivor honestly assess the need for lifestyle or spending changes in light of the reality of his or her new situation.

+ Identify immediate dire financial needs.

Help the survivor prioritize his or her financial needs, and identify those needs that will have a severe impact on the person's ability to function if not met: mortgage payments, electric bills, or food for the family. Try to cut out expenses that aren't necessary, and work on a plan to meet those that are. If disaster recovery help has been promised, quickly find out the rules and requirements for the aid. Then help the survivor through the application process.

But avoid making purchases based on the possibility of help. Rather, try to find temporary solutions that buy time while the survivor finds out the details of the aid he or she will receive.

+ Pray for the victim of the disaster and help meet real needs.

Don't hesitate to pray for the survivor. And ask if you can pray together. If the person is too distraught to identify specific prayer requests, ask God to give him or her strength to face the situation and conquer it. Also ask that God would meet the victim in the midst of this crisis and draw the person into closer relationship with and reliance on God.

You cannot meet every need of a disaster survivor. However, you can rally your church, small groups, or other friends to help meet practical needs. If you plan to help with housing or transportation, make certain that you set clear guidelines before making the offer. Clearly communicate the date when the housing help will end. All of your efforts should be focused on helping the person become self-sustaining. By clearly communicating the duration and extent of the help you're offering, you keep the long-term responsibility where it belongs—on the survivor. Your clear honesty will protect the survivor from relying on help that won't be there in the future.

+ Foster a sense of personal responsibility and determination.

The disaster survivor will have to take personal responsibility for the solution to his or her financial crisis, and he or she will have to be proactive in doing so. You can help foster a sense of personal responsibility for solving the crisis by demonstrating an active approach to problem-solving. For instance, you might download an application for food stamps, or you might highlight appropriate job openings in the classified ads. Show the person the practical—and immediate—things that he or she can do to cope with the crisis. You'll have a tough time helping a disaster survivor if you are more motivated to provide solutions than he or she is motivated to take responsibility.

Counseling Tips

After the disaster victim's immediate needs are met, he or she may still be facing a long and arduous journey ahead. The following guidelines are just a few examples of what you can do to help the person on the journey. Perhaps the most important thing you can do is dedicate yourself to supporting the person through the recovery—until the financial crisis has been adequately resolved.

+ Encourage expression of feelings.

The survivor will likely be experiencing a wide range of feelings, such as fear, anger, sadness, and vulnerability. If anxiety, depression, or anger becomes severe or debilitating, don't hesitate to seek a referral to a counselor. The strength of these emotions may be overwhelming to you, but don't respond by trying to quickly alleviate the victim's feelings. Imagine yourself in the person's position, and you may be more capable of understanding his or her feelings.

When people feel a threat to their basic security, it can be a terrifying experience. Consequently, they sometimes may blame the person or entity they believe is most responsible for their security. For many people, this may mean blaming God. Try not to judge these feelings. By allowing the victim to express fear and frustration, you can begin a dialogue about the role of faith in perseverance and recovery.

+ Help the disaster survivor create a budget.

Identify someone you know who is a successful financial planner. Get a copy of that person's budget, and use it to help the survivor plan his or her spending—or you may even want to set up a consultation with the successful financial planner. For many people, it may be important to cut up credit cards. If you're skilled in this area, help the person with the intricacies of financial planning, including areas such as consolidating debt, refinancing a house, obtaining a credit report, and buying budgeting software.

+ Help the disaster survivor find affordable and helpful professionals.

It may be important for the person to see a mental health counselor, professional financial planner, or credit counselor. Do everything you can to arrange referrals. If possible, try to assist with expenses as well.

WHEN TO REFER

Refer the disaster victim to any and all government and non-profit assistance programs you can find. Help him or her obtain and complete the necessary paperwork to apply for assistance.

You may, however, need to help the survivor find specific support and help if you notice:

+ Severe depression or anxiety. The survivor will certainly deal with sadness and anxiety. However, if the emotional impact impairs the person's ability to begin financial recovery, a referral to a psychologist or counselor is warranted. See the "When to Refer" section in the "Depression" chapter (page 44) for other signs to watch for.

+ A deeper-rooted problem caused by the financial crisis. If the financial crisis has led the survivor down the path of deeper, more destructive problems such as addictions to gambling, alcohol, drugs, or spending, discuss your concerns and refer to a counselor or a 12-step program.

+ Lack of resources. If the survivor appears to lack the skills or resources to recover, and you don't feel confident in your ability to help the person deal with the financial crisis, don't hesitate to refer to a financial planner or counselor.

Ministry Tips

+ Share the emotional and spiritual burden with the disaster victim.

Romans 12:15 says, "Be happy with those who are happy, and weep with those who weep." Emotional and spiritual support are as, if not more, important than financial help. A survivor's needs may be so great that you're tempted to keep him or her at arms' length. Realize that you can't fix the problem, but you can enter into the survivor's sorrows and successes. Rejoice with him or her when things go well, and mourn with him or her when setbacks occur. The survivor will always remember the comfort he or she found in your determination to share the burden.

+ Search your church.

Church communities can be great resources of individuals with various skills and expertise. Search your church for people willing to supply discounted (or free) services the survivor might not otherwise be able to obtain. These might include automobile repair, household maintenance, health care needs, and even haircuts. Acts 2:44-45 makes it clear that it's our duty as Christian brothers and sisters to help where and when we can during crisis.

+ Provide nonprofessional services, too.

A disaster survivor may need a place to live temporarily or may be struggling to buy groceries or other basic necessities. Offer a ride to an interview or temporary employment agency, or offer to make meals. These services are just a few examples of small but incredibly helpful things you can do to help. Be sure to offer your services and time, even if the person in need hasn't asked for assistance. The survivor may not want to be an imposition or may be too embarrassed to ask for help. Make the first move.

+ Help out financially.

Though the most obvious tip, this may be the most difficult to do. With all of our own responsibilities weighing down on us, assisting someone else financially can seem unfeasible. However, if you've prayerfully decided to do so, some suggestions include helping out with daily expenses such as groceries, or helping at an important time of year (such as giving money or gifts for Christmas or birthdays).

ADDITIONAL RESOURCES

+ Books

Blue, Ron. *Mastering Money in Your Marriage: HomeBuilders Couples Series.* Loveland, CO: FamilyLife and Group Publishing, Inc., 2000.

Dayton, Howard. *Your Money Counts: The biblical guide to earning, spending, saving, investing, giving, and getting out of debt.* Carol Stream, IL: Tyndale House Publishers, 1997.

Hood, Kregg R. *From Debt to Life: 10 Proven Steps to Beat Credit Crisis & Build Financial Freedom.* Gainesville, FL: Bridge-Logos Publishers, 2004.

+ Online Resources

www.napfa.org (The National Association of Personal Financial Advisors)

www.onepaycheckatatime.com (One Paycheck at a Time: The No-Nonsense Strategy for Becoming Debt Free)

www.crown.org (Crown Financial Ministries)

What Not to Say

+ "I wish there was something I could do."

Although this statement sounds supportive, it may be perceived as dismissive. Plus, there *are* many things you can do to help the person in crisis. Instead of this regret, ask, "What can I do to help?" When approached in a caring manner, the person may have some specific requests.

+ "You just need to get a job."

Try not to minimize the person's problems. As indicated in the previous sections, it's not always this simple. Besides, the survivor is likely already aware of the importance of a job. So instead of this non-specific suggestion, do something to help the person find a job, such as set up a meeting with a local job counselor.

+ "How did you get yourself in this situation?"

A survivor may have made some poor choices in reaction to the disaster. As you dig into the situation, you may find habits and choices that exacerbate the financial crisis brought about by the disaster. Help the survivor see how similar future choices will block his or her efforts to move forward. The only benefit of looking at past mistakes is to help the person avoid similar mistakes in the future.

+ "You just need to trust God."

It's true that the hurting person will need to trust God and his plan, but be careful not to oversimplify the situation. The survivor needs to be encouraged to actively seek solutions rather than *passively* relying on God. Instead, ask the person how you could pray for him or her. Talk about times when God has helped you through dark times. We could all learn to trust and rely on God even more. So help demonstrate or encourage this trust through your prayers and actions rather than admonitions or cursory reminders.

What to Say

+ "How are you handling this?"

By asking an open-ended question, you communicate your care and concern and give the survivor an opportunity to vent his or her frustrations or fears. You can also begin to assess a person's emotional and behavioral reactions to the crisis through the responses given.

+ "We can work through this."

By using the term *we*, you imply that you'll be there to support the disaster survivor. You also communicate a sense of hope and reframe the problem as something to be solved rather than suffered.

+ "Let's bring this to God in prayer."

With this approach, you communicate something very important: God wants to be a part of the solution. It's important to nurture this assumption early on, so it will become more natural to rely on God during the financial recovery. This statement also opens up the opportunity for intimacy and support in the form of joint prayer.

+ "What are your most pressing needs right now?"

This question has two positive effects: First, you compel the person to begin the problem-solving process by prioritizing needs. Second, you open up an opportunity to help, which is going to increase his or her sense of support and, consequently, reduce his or her sense of anxiety.

ABOUT DEBT AND BANKRUPTCY?

Scripture does not give explicit directions on bankruptcy. However, it does give clear direction on issues associated with it. Scripture shows:

✛ We are responsible to repay our debts and should do everything we can to pay them back. Romans 13:8 says, "Owe nothing to anyone—except for your obligation to love one another." Psalm 37:21 says, "The wicked borrow and never repay, but the godly are generous givers."

✛ We should avoid taking on debts that we may not be able to pay. Ecclesiastes 5:5 says, "It is better to say nothing than to make a promise and not keep it."

✛ We should get rid of debt. Proverbs 22:7 says, "Just as the rich rule the poor, so the borrower is servant to the lender."

Scripture does not explicitly call bankruptcy a sin. It appears, however, that we should strive to find every other possible option. There are some significant practical downsides to bankruptcy. A bankruptcy usually remains on a credit report for 10 years and makes future borrowing at reasonable interest rates very difficult. Landlords and employers may also reject an applicant or candidate based on the "mark" of bankruptcy they find in the application process.

Some forms of bankruptcy (such as Chapter 13) provide a level of financial and legal protection while the filer works to develop a reorganization and repayment plan.

CHAPTER SIX

Stress and Anxiety
Helping Survivors Cope With Stress

Erin is a 36-year-old wife and mother of two. She met her husband, Mike, just after college, and they have been married for 12 years. Their children are Jake, 9, and Amber, 6. Erin also has a successful career as a public relations director for a local division of a national ministry.

She loves her job, but she's found that juggling her roles of wife and mother with the demands of her job is increasingly challenging and stressful. Erin drops her kids off at school early each morning, and a sitter picks them up in the afternoon and stays with them until Erin or Mike arrives home from work. By the time she finishes with dinner, homework, and baths for the kids, Erin rarely makes it to bed before 11:00 p.m.

Finding time for her relationship with Mike has been hard, and finding time for herself (devotional time, exercise) has been completely squeezed out of her schedule. She no longer attends her Saturday morning women's group at the church because even when she isn't working, the household chores have piled up. She misses the support and friendship of the group, but tells herself she will start back up when things at work slow down.

Several weeks ago, a series of tornadoes struck the area where Erin and Mike live. Erin was at work when the storms started in the late afternoon.

She wasn't able to reach the sitter who had picked the kids up at school. So in spite of warnings from her co-workers, she tried to drive home. With the storm raging and a downpour of blinding rain, Erin couldn't see where she was going. Neither could anyone else, and that's when the accident happened. Erin was taken to the emergency room. Thankfully, everyone in the accident suffered only minor injuries. But it was several hours before she was able to make contact with Mike and the kids and to determine that they were all safe.

In addition, the storms did extensive damage to their home and personal belongings. The damage was so extensive that they are unable to live in their house. They are hopeful that their homeowner's insurance will allow them to do the necessary repairs, but the claims are so backed up they are not sure when their payments will come through. In the meantime, they have moved in with Mike's brother, his wife, and their three children.

Erin was raised in a Christian home and has a strong faith in Jesus. She and Mike are members of a large local church and attend regularly. She prayed fervently for her family's safety during the storms and has been grateful to God for their safety.

But in the days following the storm, Erin has been unable to sleep and has experienced frequent nightmares about the storms. She dreams that her children or Mike has been injured or killed. As weeks have passed, Erin's struggles have become more significant. She finds herself unable to concentrate or focus at work. She is extremely irritable and finds herself snapping at the kids and even her co-workers. Erin attributes all of this to the stress of not being in her home and having to live with Mike's family.

She has also found herself struggling to pray and feels angry toward God about their personal losses. Problems with contractors and the insurance settlement have left Mike and Erin with no idea of when they might be able to move home. They're looking at options for moving into an apartment temporarily, but are not sure if they can afford this.

Erin feels angry and sometimes hopeless about their situation, but she also feels guilty since she knows others lost much more. She has friends and co-workers whose homes were completely destroyed. Some people even died in the storm. Her guilt has made her reluctant to talk about her feelings.

Plus, Erin hasn't really reached out for help. With her intense schedule the past few years, she has lost touch with or become distant from many of her close friends. Her family lives in another part of the country, and while they have supported her with phone calls and prayers, they have been unable to visit.

Then, last week while driving home from work, Erin had an attack. She felt tightness and pain in her chest and found it difficult to breathe. Her heart raced wildly and she broke out in a cold sweat. She was trembling so hard that she had to pull off the road and call Mike. She felt faint and overwhelmed by a terrible feeling. Erin was convinced she was having a heart attack.

Mike and a family member rushed Erin to a local emergency room. After examination by a physician and a series of tests, the doctor assured Erin that she had not experienced a heart attack. While he recommended that Erin follow up with her family doctor for some more tests, he believed that Erin had experienced a panic attack.

SCRIPTURE HELP

+ **Deuteronomy 31:8**
+ **Psalm 34:4**
+ **Psalm 139:23-24**
+ **Proverbs 12:25**
+ **Isaiah 26:3**

+ **Matthew 6:25-34**
+ **Mark 4:38-39**
+ **John 16:33**
+ **Philippians 4:4-9**
+ **1 Timothy 4:13-15**

ADDITIONAL RESOURCES

+ **Books**

Hart, Archibald. *The Anxiety Cure: You Can Find Emotional Tranquillity and Wholeness.* Nashville, TN: Word Publishing, 1999.

Care and Counseling Tips

THE BASICS

Stress and anxiety are normal parts of our human experience. God programmed us with a "stress response" to situations that are dangerous or life-threatening. However, events can cause this normal stress response to become pathological.

A constant state of stress can be physically and psychologically damaging. In our society, many people live stress-filled daily lives that push their coping mechanisms to the max as they struggle to meet work, family, financial, and church obligations.

Then, when a crisis or disaster occurs, these stressed individuals may not have the emotional, physical, and spiritual resources available to cope with the trauma. These incidents can push already stressed individuals into post-traumatic stress disorder, panic disorder, or other anxiety-related problems if not addressed right away.

Care Tips

+ Evaluate lifestyle. Help crisis survivors evaluate their stress levels, their support systems, their lifestyles, and their spiritual practices to see where they may need help. With the high levels of stress most people carry in their daily lives, many have no margin to cope with the added stress of a crisis or disaster. Providing education about good self-care and stress management will not only help them through the time of crisis but will also help them manage stress in the future.

+ Promote health. It's critical for survivors to practice good self-care in the aftermath of trauma. Diet, exercise, and sleep patterns can support a person's ability to manage stress or can contribute to problems and even trigger panic attacks. While it's not your role to nag the survivor about lifestyle issues, you can encourage the survivor to take a healthy lifestyle approach to minimize additional stress. Survivors should make an effort to eat healthy foods in the days and weeks following a disaster. They shouldn't skip or miss meals and should limit or avoid consumption of sweets, caffeine, and alcohol. Exercise, even moderate walking, can also help to combat stress.

+ Encourage support systems. Survivors of a crisis or disaster need immediate emotional and spiritual support. They need someone to talk with who makes them feel safe to express feelings of fear, anger, sadness, or loss. Have a list of the names and numbers of the disaster relief organizations that will be in your area, and make that information available to survivors. Help them find the support they need.

Counseling Tips

+ Use prayer and Christian meditation.

Many Christians may fear the term *meditation* because they associate it with the New Age movement or eastern religions. However, to many, Christian meditation is simply taking focused quiet time to listen to God. It can be a form of spiritual rest. It can be a time to pray, offer praise, or reflect on Scripture. Dr. Archibald Hart writes extensively about Christian meditation in his book *The Anxiety Cure*. He indicates that Christian meditation can help in the recovery from anxiety and anxiety disorders.

+ Make short-term changes to manage stress.

It's important for survivors of crisis and disaster to, at least temporarily, cut back on their work and life responsibilities. It's normal for anyone who has experienced a crisis or trauma to go through a time when their capacity to perform at work, church, or home is compromised. Asking for help can be difficult, but encourage survivors to give themselves time to recover from the stress of the crisis before resuming a full schedule.

+ Help them understand a "crisis of faith."

It's not uncommon for Christians to experience a "crisis of faith" following a crisis or disaster. Survivors may find it difficult to pray or might even have feelings of anger at God. They may stop going to church. It's important to normalize this experience for survivors. See Chapter 1 for how to help.

+ Promote gratitude.

Gently point out the positive aspects in life, the gifts God has given us. In the face of a disaster, people often lose touch with the blessings they have experienced. Encourage survivors to keep a "gratitude journal." Each day, they can list the things they are grateful for that day, even if all they write is being grateful for a relaxing cup of tea or a favorite television program. The process will begin to create a more hopeful mindset.

What Not to Say

+ "Just calm down."

This kind of statement indicates to survivors that they should have control over their feelings of stress and anxiety. In reality, stress and anxiety are normal symptoms of post-traumatic stress. These symptoms are also not simply psychological or emotional. They have a biological and physiological basis. Anxiety is caused by a biochemical change in the brain. This change is triggered by a crisis, and it can take time (days, weeks, or months) for balance to be re-established. In most people, this will happen normally, but some may need counseling or medication.

+ "Have more faith."

While faith may be shaken following times of crisis, simply telling people to have more faith or trust God will not be helpful in reducing stress or helping them resolve their anger with God. Allowing them to be angry, scared, or upset without judgment is the most helpful attitude you can take. When your relationships sufficiently develop, you can gently introduce statements that remind survivors of God's love.

What to Say

+ "You're having a normal response to an abnormal event."

It's necessary to help survivors normalize the emotional, physical, behavioral, and spiritual symptoms they have after a crisis. If they can understand that many of the symptoms they're experiencing are normal, they can feel more relaxed and not that they're "going crazy."

+ "What are some practical ways we can reduce your stress right now?"

Brainstorm ways to help reduce the daily stress load of the survivor, and take practical steps to intervene. Helping to run errands, prepare meals, or watch children can take a huge weight off of the survivor's mind. But make sure you and your volunteers set healthy boundaries and implement them.

+ "Tell me about what you're afraid of or worried about."

Often a crisis event can trigger feelings of fear or vulnerability. Even if survivors weren't seriously injured, the very thought that they could have been hurt or killed can trigger intense fears. Encourage survivors to discuss their fears and concerns about personal safety or the safety of their loved ones.

WHEN TO REFER

The following are normal symptoms of post-traumatic stress:

+ **anger**
+ **irritability**
+ **anxiety**
+ **fear**
+ **confusion**
+ **inability to concentrate**
+ **preoccupation with or obsessions about the event**
+ **sleep disturbance or nightmares**
+ **withdrawal**
+ **crying spells**
+ **headaches**
+ **fatigue**

If these symptoms don't get better or if they get worse within about 30 days, then you should refer the survivor to a professional therapist for evaluation. If symptoms persist beyond three months, a survivor might be suffering from post-traumatic stress disorder.

An anxiety disorder is distinguished from normal anxiety by the intensity and frequency of the anxiety, the severity of impairment, and how long the anxiety has been a problem. A clinical diagnosis of any mental disorder is based on a number of symptoms, and only a licensed professional should make a diagnosis. The following signs may indicate an anxiety disorder:

+ **Post-traumatic stress symptoms persist for more than three months or get worse after one month.**
+ **The person experiences a panic attack.**
+ **The person has suicidal thoughts.**

CHAPTER SEVEN

Managing Expectations
Helping Survivors Know What to Expect

On the second anniversary of 9/11, at Ground Zero, I gave out water, water, and more water. And I greeted hundreds of people.

Just then a hotel manager made a beeline for me—he saw my red Salvation Army jacket with the Emergency Disaster Services logo on my back. He quickly explained his dilemma: "I have two housekeepers, Kathy and Donna, who need help. Do whatever you can to help them. They were working the day of the attack. Now they're having problems. Will you please help them? I'll put any resources at your disposal that you need."

These two women thought they had moved beyond the horrific attack on the World Trade Center towers two years earlier. But on the morning of this anniversary, they both woke up feeling more like victims than survivors, nearly paralyzed with fear. They tried to act normally around their families and somehow managed to go to work "as usual."

Kathy and Donna were thankful to finally have their jobs back. The hotel they worked in was across the street from Ground Zero. Once it was determined that the hotel would be able to reopen, the management asked all employees to wait for the reopening and to rejoin their team. But it had taken far longer to get it back up and running than they had expected;

employees had to go for well over a year without work. Kathy and Donna assumed that during that long time off they had already recovered from the shock of what they had experienced.

They assumed that they could go back to life as "normal." After all, they were still alive, none of their loved ones had died, and they were now back among their old colleagues doing jobs they knew and enjoyed. They even worked with the same supervisors and manager.

But that day, with all of the anniversary ceremonies held just outside their hotel, they found themselves reliving their 9/11 experiences over and over. They were having flashbacks—a very common experience faced by disaster survivors.

I asked another volunteer to go with me. She joined me to pray while I talked with the women.

Once the four of us had introduced ourselves and were settled into a comfortable room, I asked Kathy and Donna to tell me their stories.

Kathy: "I'm seeing it all again. Every time I close my eyes, I see it all again…I see the bodies…I can still see that plaid shirt and cargo pants that one person wore. Another one was in a pinstriped suit. Why am I reliving this? Why isn't this over?"

Donna: "I shouldn't have worn these shoes. They're the same ones I wore that day. When I realized what was happening, I started running. I ran all the way to the bridge, across the bridge, and on to home. I ran for miles and miles. I learned then that these shoes kill my feet when I run in them; I had huge blisters that night. Why did I wear them again today, of all days?"

They didn't understand that shoes, and clothes, could bring back memories. And they didn't understand why they were not yet "over" what had happened.

They needed to break the cycle of fear they were traveling.

As they told me their stories, they repeatedly said, "Oh, Jesus, help me."

I asked them if they believed in Jesus, if they believed in his Word. They each answered in the affirmative. So I asked them to act on that belief each time they started having flashbacks.

"But how do I do that? I don't know how to stop thinking about it once I start." I encouraged them to focus on God's promises in his Word rather than on their fears. Together we began to read Psalm 46:

"God is our refuge and strength,
>   Always ready to help in times of trouble.
So we will not fear when earthquakes come
>   And the mountains crumble into the sea."

"Do you believe that God is your refuge and strength?" I asked.

"Yes."

"Then each time you begin to have a flashback, make a decision. Decide that you will focus on God's strength and the fact that he is with you in times of trouble. Can you memorize this verse so that you can repeat it when you need to? It will help you to focus on him, not on your memories."

That was a new idea to them. It helped them get out of the ruts of the thought patterns they felt stuck in. They now had something to focus on other than their memories. And it helped them to know that with God's help they had the power to overcome their fears.

By the time we parted, they felt confident that they could last through the day's work. They knew that the Lord would be with them and would give them strength. And they had the hope that their memories would no longer have overwhelming power over them.

SCRIPTURE HELP

+ **Psalm 40**
+ **Psalm 46**
+ **Proverbs 14:30**
+ **Ecclesiastes 3:1-8**
+ **Lamentations 3:21-26**

+ **Matthew 6:25-34**
+ **John 14:1**
+ **Galatians 5:22-25**
+ **James 3:14-18**

Care and Counseling Tips

THE BASICS

Most survivors expect life to reorder itself quickly; they anticipate that they will be able to resume their old lives in short order. They expect to rebuild their lives quickly. When that doesn't happen, they sometimes become angry at others for not helping them enough. How can you encourage them to manage these expectations in a healthy manner?

Each encounter takes wisdom and prayer. Help survivors understand that even if things aren't happening when and how they expected, things are moving forward.

If the survivors are Christians, then God's Word should be an authority in their lives. A passage that many already know is Proverbs 3:5-6: "Trust in the Lord with all your heart; do not depend on your own understanding. Seek his will in all you do, and he will show you which path to take."

Encourage them to recall this when they're disappointed that healing isn't happening when and how they want.

Care Tips

+ **Listen.** Do far more listening than speaking.

+ **Make lists.** Encourage survivors to write things down. Help them make lists of the tasks they need to accomplish, in the order the tasks need to be addressed. Encourage them to write down their frustrations and their accomplishments. This will give them the assurance that things are changing, are getting done.

+ **Be realistic.** Help survivors determine what realistic expectations look like. There may be an official who can help them understand what governmental help is available, and when they can expect it.

+ **Encourage healthy routines.** Encourage them to get into a regular routine or schedule as soon as possible. Specifically encourage them to eat regularly and rest well. Everyone needs rest. (You do, and so do those you are serving.)

Counseling Tips

+ Listen. Encourage survivors to tell their stories. Don't stop them from telling you the same story more than once.

+ Repeat back. Paraphrase what you hear. Summarizing what you are hearing will allow you to confirm that you have understood what was said.

+ Don't interrupt. Again, listen more than you talk. (We can't stress that enough.)

+ Ask simple questions. Survivors often have trouble thinking clearly. If your question is complex, they may not understand what you're asking. This could make them feel that they have even less control than they actually do.

+ Be willing to be still. If the survivor doesn't feel like talking, be willing to just be with him or her. Your presence may help the survivor to find peace and comfort in waiting.

+ Don't make promises you can't keep. Don't promise that things will move quickly or smoothly. But do help survivors see which practical steps they can take to get or keep things moving.

+ Don't try to be a hero. Don't try to solve their problems. Instead, help survivors to find answers and assistance.

+ Help with records. Encourage survivors to document promised delivery time frames; this will help them remember when they should realistically expect help instead of becoming impatient when things don't happen immediately.

+ Encourage. Encourage survivors to take part in activities that they enjoy and where they have some degree of control, such as exercise or church groups. This will help them to keep from being quite so frustrated with processes they don't have control over.

WHEN TO REFER

+ When the survivor has practical, physical needs that aren't being met. Make certain that survivors are connected to the people and agencies that can help. (When you first arrive on the scene, find out which agencies are helping in which capacities.) If they have physical needs following a massive disaster, make certain they have registered with the local CAN—the Coordinated Assistance Network. Once they have signed up with one participating agency, they automatically have access to all other agencies in the network without having to register with each one individually.

+ Look for physical symptoms. If survivors are having difficulty sleeping or concentrating, or if they are having consistent headaches, irregular breathing, heart palpitations, or digestive problems, suggest that they see a doctor.

+ Address spiritual needs. If you are not in your home community, refer survivors to a local church that is prepared to and can provide ongoing spiritual support.

Ministry Tips

+ Encourage expression. Encourage survivors to express their anger, doubts, and frustrations in healthy ways. Encourage them to write down their feelings and observations. This will give them an outlet for frustration and will help them to see progress.

+ Avoid shallow answers. Don't give pat answers to spiritual questions. Instead, encourage survivors to search for their own answers, and offer to help. Finding meaning in what they have experienced is key to their moving on with life.

+ Don't insist. Don't push survivors to believe exactly what you believe; their faith must be their own. Encourage them to recall what they've based their faith on in the past. If they believe in the Bible, help them recall some of their favorite passages. Then ask them how those passages have helped them in the past. Ask them if they still believe those words; encourage them to allow the words to guide them.

+ Plan ahead. Understand potential trigger events. Anniversaries often trigger memories. Help them to plan for those events.

What Not to Say

+ "It's God's will."
This can sometimes cause people to respond with more anger toward God and sets up more distance between them and God.

+ "Stop worrying."
This directive, as we all know, is easier said than done. Don't place impossible demands on a disaster survivor.

+ "It will be OK."
Life will never be the same for this person again. So "OK" will look different in the future.

+ "I know how you feel."
You may have empathy for what has happened to this person, but you do not know exactly how he or she is feeling. Don't lessen the validity of the survivor's feelings.

+ "Life goes on."
Avoid clichés like this. Clichés diminish a person's rightful feelings and make you seem callous and uncaring.

What to Say

+ "May I pray for you?"
This allows them to give you permission to pray for them. It also assures them that someone is interceding on their behalf, even if they can't yet pray for themselves.

+ "I'm so sorry."
This acknowledges that they have experienced something that would hurt others, too. It shows that you care without blaming anyone.

+ "My heart goes out to you. You have my sympathy."
This acknowledges that their story has touched your heart, and that they aren't alone in feeling pain.

+ "What can I do to help?"
This affirms that they aren't alone. It acknowledges that they can ask others for help.

ADDITIONAL RESOURCES

+ Books

Koenig, Harold G., M.D. *In the Wake of Disaster: Religious Responses to Terrorism and Catastrophe.* West Conshohocken, PA: Templeton Foundation Press, 2006.

Pastoral Crisis Intervention Course Workbook. Ellicott City, MD: International Critical Incident Stress Foundation, 2005.

Roberts, Rabbi Stephen B., and Rev. Willard W. C. Ashley Sr., eds. *Disaster Spiritual Care: Practical Clergy Responses to Community, Regional and National Tragedy.* Woodstock, Vermont: SkyLight Paths Publishing, 2008.

+ Books to Give Away

Beside Quiet Waters: Help for Overcoming Anxiety by International Bible Society—Send the Light (a small booklet addressing anxiety).

When Your Whole World Changes by International Bible Society—Send the Light (a 30-day reading plan with journal space).

Submitted by: Sues Hyde, IBS-STL, Director of Outreach.

CHAPTER EIGHT

People at Risk

Assisting Survivors in Special Circumstances

Edith lives alone in Mississippi, in the house where she grew up. She's in her later 80s and has trouble walking and difficulty seeing, especially at night. Her daughter lives almost 600 miles away and isn't able to visit often.

Edith likes the comfort and privacy of her own home and dreads the thought of leaving for any reason. When she must go out, Edith relies upon friends in the neighborhood to take her to doctor visits and to the grocery store.

Life is hard even when the weather is good, but Edith worries about what she will do when the storms come during hurricane season. During the last storm, her telephone went out for three days, and she wasn't able to speak with anyone.

The thought of having to spend her days and nights in a shelter with people she doesn't know terrifies Edith. She can't imagine how she would cope in such a strange environment.

All across the country, scenarios like Edith's play out again and again. Shortly after Hurricane Katrina, a Kaiser Family Foundation Poll asked those who didn't evacuate this question: "Which was the biggest reason you did not leave?" Of those polled, 22 percent said that they were physically unable to leave, and another 23 percent said that they needed to stay to take care of someone who was physically unable to evacuate.

These statistics are a frightening reminder that within any community, there is a significant percentage of the population who cannot or will not evacuate in times of disaster. There are those who are at risk due to a mental, physical, or emotional condition that diminishes their ability or desire to react quickly and decisively during a crisis.

Without assistance—possibly your help—their very lives are at risk.

SCRIPTURE HELP

+ **Psalm 10:14**
+ **Matthew 14:14-16**
+ **Luke 10:33-35**
+ **2 Corinthians 1:2-4**
+ **Philippians 2:1-3**

Care and Counseling Tips

THE BASICS

Emergency management professionals list several groups of people as being "at risk" in times of disaster. Most notably, that list includes:

- senior citizens, particularly those suffering from mental or physical difficulties;
- people with disabilities that impact their ability to react;
- the poor, especially those dependent upon community infrastructures;
- children;
- the homeless.

+ Don't generalize. People in the above groups are not necessarily "alike," nor do they have the same needs. Even within each of these categories, the differences and challenges can be vastly different from person to person. Although there may be some similarities, each group has unique characteristics and challenges that place them at risk when disasters affect their communities.

+ Avoid stereotypes. When generalities are applied to those at risk, there can be great offense taken at the thought of being "lumped in" with "special needs." Even the term "special needs" can be offensive and should be avoided as a term to describe a particular group.

Care Tips

Recognize that some seniors and people with disabilities may need extra assistance in times of disasters. Your willingness to help can make all the difference in the world. Use the following suggestions for specific groups.

+ Senior citizens. Consider that for senior citizens, there may be mobility issues or periodic confusion, and quite possibly, the need for access to medications and medical durable goods. Many seniors would rather remain at home than go to a shelter. But often at home, they are unprepared to "shelter-in-place," having an inadequate supply of basic necessities. Also, seniors may have no way of getting to a shelter and may not want to ask for help. Offering to transport someone to a shelter can be the deciding factor in whether the person stays or goes.

+ People with physical disabilities. Those with physical disabilities face particular challenges in the aftermath of a disaster. For example, the visually impaired may be reluctant to leave their familiar surroundings. Their ability to move about and to function is often diminished in unfamiliar surroundings. Their service animal may become confused or disoriented due to the disruption of the regular routine. For someone with these challenges, planning prior to a disaster and assistance during the event can make a huge difference.

Those who are hearing impaired may need assistance in getting information on impending disasters and what to do after the event. Those with mobility issues may require assistance getting to and even into the shelter.

+ Those who don't speak English. Disaster survivors who don't speak English will need translation services and may need special assistance to understand what to do and where to go after a disaster.

+ Parents. Parents hopefully will have talked to their children about what to do in case of an emergency. Day-care and school lockdown and pickup information will hopefully be announced on radio and television following a disaster. But parents will most likely be terribly upset until they can reach their children and know that they're safe. Be available to relay official information as quickly as possible to such parents.

+ Those with dietary restrictions. People with dietary restrictions will need to make every effort to have special food on hand or with them, as such items may not be available in a shelter or a store if deliveries are disrupted. If such dietary restrictions pose an immediate health risk, act as a liaison with health professionals operating in the area.

+ Those with dementia. Certainly, those with dementia and extreme confusion should be registered with the Alzheimer's Association Safe Return Program or a similar program run by a reputable disaster organization.

PREPAREDNESS INITIATIVES

FOR SENIORS AND PEOPLE WITH DISABILITIES

In most communities, those who need special assistance can register with the office of emergency services or the local fire department so help can be provided when needed. There are a variety of "preparedness initiatives" that are designed to help seniors and people with disabilities make it through times of crisis.

+ The Salvation Army is committed to meeting the needs of those affected by disaster, and has recently developed a program called "Preparing Together." This program places a senior or person with a disability with a volunteer who becomes a "preparedness coach" to ensure that the proper steps are taken during a disaster and to assist with family contacts and evacuation at the time of a disaster. Preparedness coaches visit the people they are looking after about three or four times a year and provide assurance that they will do whatever they can to help should a disaster strike.

The preparedness tool used in the program provides emergency management with important information, including but not limited to doctors' names, medication, and family contacts. The guide is displayed in the home and can give emergency responders vital information.

Churches, civic groups and clubs, and disaster service agencies are being encouraged to utilize this program within the respective communities they serve.

+ The Alzheimer's Association, recognizing the need to provide a safety net for those suffering from Alzheimer's disease, has teamed up with the MedicAlert Foundation to create a partnership called MedicAlert + Alzheimer's Association Safe Return.

The "Safe Return" program offers assistance when a person wanders off or is lost, while providing access to vital medical information when needed. When a person with dementia wanders or becomes lost, one call immediately activates a community support network to help reunite the lost person with his or her caregiver. There is a toll-free 24-hour emergency number that any citizen or first responder can call to help reunite the individual with family or caregivers. The nearest Alzheimer's Association office provides support during search and rescue efforts.

+ Government agencies. FEMA has excellent information on their website, found at www.fema.gov. Once there, click on "More Audiences…" and then on the link to "Individuals with Special Needs." Another good source of information is www.disabilityinfo.gov.

WHEN TO REFER

Members of at-risk populations will need special attention and care following a disaster. For them, even the change in routine can be especially upsetting and dangerous. Trauma counselors, medical advisors, and social workers will all be helpful in assisting these survivors and should be consulted proactively.

Counseling Tips

+ Be supportive. Understand that those "at risk" may not feel that they deserve help and may not want to "be a burden" to those who want to help. The fear of the unknown may be overwhelming to the point that it creates a paralysis in their ability to act decisively.

+ Be an advocate. As an advocate, your willingness to reach out to family members to assure them that their loved one is safe and secure brings a sense of peace to both the senior or person with a disability and to the family members. Communicating the well-being of a loved one before, during, and after a disaster event can bring great comfort to the family.

+ Be respectful. Look beyond the survivor's mental confusion or physical disability. Those you're caring for are individuals who need your respect and care, not your pity and charity.

AFTER THE DISASTER

+ Check for hazards in the home. Many seniors and some people with certain disabilities rely upon the familiarity of their surroundings to function well. During a disaster, familiar objects may be broken or missing. Such changes can create hazards that increase the chance for serious accidents and additional confusion once the survivor returns home. Go through the home with the survivor, and note changes. Together, plan a new routine that incorporates the changes. If possible, enlist the aid of family members or friends to check on the survivor in the first few weeks following a disaster or until a new routine can be established.

+ Be prepared for the future. Help the survivor make his or her home as safe as possible for the future. Doing so will not only help ensure the well-being of the survivor but will also instill confidence that the survivor will be well prepared for any future event. Make sure that halls and doorways are free of clutter that would block a quick escape from the home. Check bookcases, hanging pictures, and overhead lights, all items that could fall in an earthquake or flood and block an escape path.

+ Make an evacuation plan. The key to evacuation is to have a plan. A preparedness partner is a must, as confusion, lack of motivation, and a general sense of unwillingness to leave the home can negatively impact a successful evacuation. Enlist the aid of the survivor's family members, neighbors, friends, or church members.

You don't want to frighten the survivor by dwelling on the possibility of another disaster. Instead, encourage the survivor that being prepared for an emergency, whether it's a disaster or just a big snowstorm, can help him or her feel confident, strong, and able to face any situation.

(continued from previous page)

Go over the following checklist with the survivor, and help him or her take the following steps.

- Create a network of neighbors, relatives, and friends to aid you in an emergency.
- Have alternate evacuation routes because some roads may be closed or blocked in a disaster.
- List the type and model numbers of all personal medical devices.
- Make sure caregivers know how to operate durable medical equipment.
- Keep specialized items ready, including extra wheelchair batteries, oxygen, catheters, medication, prescriptions, food for service animals, and any other items you might need. Be sure to make provisions for medications that require refrigeration.
- Wear medical alert tags or bracelets to identify your disability.
- Preplan for the access and availability of more than one facility if you are dependent on a dialysis machine or other life-sustaining equipment or treatment.

What Not to Say

+ **"The same thing happened to my sister."**
Those in distress want you to listen and focus on *their* emotions; telling your own stories suggests that their difficulties are "no big deal." Also, your credibility diminishes when you turn the attention back on yourself, rather than staying focused on them.

+ **"God won't give you more than you can handle."**
Avoid clichés and potentially challenging statements. These statements may pose more questions than they provide reassuring thought. They may suggest or infer that there is blame and punishment involved.

+ **"Older people are better prepared to face disasters because they've been through so much more."**
Disasters create challenges for everyone, at every stage of life. Singling out a segment of the population can make those people feel undervalued.

What to Say

+ "Please know that I am here for you."

Simple statements that demonstrate your concern and genuine care will go a long way to putting someone at ease. Many emotional and spiritual care providers use the "ministry of presence," the act of being mentally, physically, and spiritually with someone in an attitude of care and compassion that transcends mere words.

+ "Tell me what happened to you."

People who have just been through a disaster need an opportunity to tell their stories. More than anything, they often need to express what they're feeling so that you can hopefully affirm that their reactions are normal and appropriate.

+ "Can I pray?"

Take the person aside and quietly ask if you can pray right there. If the survivor agrees, ask God for peace and strength during this difficult time, and thank him for his love.

CHAPTER NINE

Isolation and Loss of Support System
Nurturing the Bereft

The morning hours of May 22nd seemed like any other in the northern Colorado town of Windsor. A little cloudier than usual, a little breezier, with an odd heaviness to the air.

But it was nothing that alarmed Jacque as she went about her morning routine. Having returned from teaching early classes at the gym, she set about straightening up the small house she shared with Jim, her husband, and Tails, her dog.

As the morning progressed, the breeze picked up considerably, and it began to sprinkle. And then the morning suddenly tore apart.

It began to rain in earnest, and within minutes to hail. The hail became intense—golf-ball size. The power went out. The sky grew so dark that, without electricity, it seemed like night. All this happened within a matter of minutes.

Jacque looked out the window, wondering, "Where did a big storm like this come from in such a hurry?" Windsor sits just on the edge of the Colorado plains, and usually residents there can see storms coming in from over the mountains to the west.

But for this storm there was no warning. Because this storm was a massive tornado, and Jacque's house sat directly in its path.

"When I looked out, I didn't even realize it was a tornado. It got really still and it was so dark, but I didn't see a funnel cloud, so it didn't register right away."

But when Jacque saw a railroad car across the field from her house slowly rise from the ground and begin to turn in midair, it finally hit her. "I screamed for the dog, and then realized I didn't know what to do. We didn't have a basement; there was no time to leave the house. So I grabbed my cell phone and Tails, and we hid under the bed. I didn't know what else to do."

As they cowered on the floor, the queen-size bed their only protection, Jacque said the pressure in her ears became so intense that she thought her eardrums would burst. Tails whined and shook, and Jacque covered him with her body.

"What they say about a tornado sounding like a freight train is true. First there's deadly silence, and then there's this deafening roar," she said. "I heard the house being torn up, and windows breaking, and furniture hitting the bed and the walls. Then I felt a huge rush of air. I guess that was the roof blowing off."

And then it was over.

But in a way, another storm was just beginning.

"When Tails and I crawled out from under the bed, I couldn't believe it. The walls of my house were still standing, miraculously. But the roof was gone, the windows were gone, the furniture was either broken to bits or gone. Except for the bed. I know God saved me. There's no doubt in my mind at all."

When she looked outside, Jacque saw that the roof had landed on her car. Most of the trees in her yard were snapped like sticks. Debris was everywhere. Her entire neighborhood looked like the aftermath of a huge explosion.

With shaking hands, she tried to call her husband, but cell phone signals were out. "I just stood there shaking. I couldn't reach Jim. I didn't know if he was OK. Even if my car hadn't been under a tree, there was so much debris in the street I couldn't have driven away. We were new to the area, so there were no family members to call, even if the phone had been working. I felt utterly alone."

Within an hour or so, even while residents were just venturing out from what was left of their houses, people in Jacque's neighborhood were ordered to evacuate because of ruptured gas lines.

"So I took Tails and just walked away, over and around the rubble. I went several blocks to the library and sat on a bench. Finally, my phone worked and I left a message for my husband where I was. Turns out he was trying to get into Windsor to find me, but they had most of the roads blocked."

But Colorado still has lots of dirt back roads, and Jim finally wound his way into town and to the library. "That was the best hug I've ever had," Jacque remembered.

From there, the little family checked into a local motel. "My mom in Oregon sent us money to stay in a motel for a few weeks until we could figure out the insurance stuff." Jacque's gym had been hit, so she couldn't go to work. Her neighbors had been evacuated, so she had no idea where they were or if they were OK.

"It was just so isolating. It was days before we were allowed back into our neighborhood. We had no family nearby to turn to. We didn't know what had happened to our neighbors and friends. I couldn't go to work. I had no car, except when my husband wasn't working. I felt so alone."

Of course, Jacque is grateful to be alive. But fear still plagues her even now. "Things are pretty much back to normal," she said. "But sometimes a fear of the future will just wash over me. I picture standing in my destroyed house, all alone, and I get depressed and scared. And then I feel guilty, because all I lost were material things.

"But still, I hope the fear goes away someday."

Care and Counseling Tips

THE BASICS

So much can be taken from an individual in one act of nature or man. Some people lose their parents or children, others lose their friends or homes, and others lose their sense of security or important links in the community.

A heavy sense of isolation sets in as the life they knew will never be the same. Loved ones in other areas may not fully understand, and loved ones nearby may have lost their ability to help. As you reach out to a disaster survivor who has lost his or her support system, remember the following:

+ Isolation breeds isolation. The more alone a person feels, the more he or she will withdraw from supporting relationships. And most people don't know how to respond to a person who withdraws and isolates. You may be frustrated with how easily the disaster survivor seems to give up or the resistance he or she seems to show to your efforts for relationship. Remember that the survivor's reaction is more about the grief and pain he or she is going through than feelings or thoughts about you.

+ You can't drag someone out of grief or isolation. You can invite, encourage, reach out to, support, call, and visit. But you can't force someone out of his or her grief. Continue to hold the door open and point a way out of isolation and depression, but ultimately the person will have to make the effort to step out. Your encouragement and support can be the lifeline that helps the person find his or her way out of isolation.

+ Losing part or all of your support system is terrifying and lonely. The person, system, or community whom the survivor relied on for comfort is gone. While you cannot replace what has been lost, you can be one facet of the new support system he or she needs.

Care Tips

+ Offer to listen.

Isolation and withdrawal are the enemies of healthy grief. A person who has experienced loss or trauma needs to talk about the experience. Honestly and gently communicate to the disaster survivor that he or she needs to talk about what happened to keep moving through the grief. Let the person know that you want to hear about his or her feelings and experiences, even if it feels repetitious.

+ Spend time with the person.

Stop by the person's house, send an e-mail, or make a phone call. Your efforts in connecting with the person will serve as a reminder that your relationship remains intact. Your unconditional positive regard, warmth, and empathy will speak volumes to the person when he or she is feeling isolated.

But avoid the trap of taking complete responsibility for the person's emotional health. You can and should be supportive. But you shouldn't give in to internal pressure to fulfill unrealistic expectations. The disaster survivor can become emotionally dependent on you, which in the long term will hinder his or her recovery. Resist the urge to flee the relationship, but set up healthy limits and boundaries.

+ Help the person identify and utilize agencies and organizations that will help meet practical needs.

Help the survivor identify governmental and nonprofit organizations that can help with immediate needs. Then accompany him or her through the application process. Your presence may serve as an automatic reference and endorsement that some agencies are looking for when deciding if and how they will help. Your support will also help the person know that he or she is not alone.

+ If appropriate, help the disaster survivor find purpose through helping others.

A person who has suffered serious loss in a disaster needs your help coping with grief and loss. But if possible and appropriate, a person struggling with isolation can benefit greatly from helping others.

Studies indicate that there are tremendous health benefits to serving, including lowering depression and despair. It may seem counterintuitive to have a disaster victim reach out to others in service. However, serving others leads to a number of positive circumstances:

- It provides an opportunity to meet new people, create new networks, and build new relationships.
- It takes the focus off of loss and brings attention back to hope.
- It empowers the person who serves to feel value and purpose.

If appropriate, invite the disaster survivor to join you the next time your organization or church goes out to serve others. The victim's own pain and loss will likely give him or her greater compassion and empathy for those he or she serves.

+ Help the survivor begin a new support system.

Even after loss, new support systems can begin. The disaster survivor can start to build vital relationships through support groups, small groups at church, distant family members, friends, co-workers, and therapists or other professionals. Encourage the survivor to pursue such channels in an effort to build new relationships. Make a list of numbers and services available in the area, and offer to help the survivor connect with groups or organizations that can be of service.

Counseling Tips

+ Meet emotional needs through physical activity.

Loneliness and isolation have been proven to exacerbate heart disease, cancer, and other life-threatening sicknesses. Physical exercise not only combats some of these diseases but has also been proven to help with depression. Meeting for coffee or a meal is a great way to connect with an isolated or lonely person. Meeting for a walk, jog, or bike ride is an even better approach. If you can't personally join the survivor, try to provide names and numbers of resources that can help the person meet others and get started on an exercise-based program.

Physical activity gives the disaster survivor a reason to connect beyond talking about difficulties. It also provides an enjoyable experience, a shared hobby or common connection with you, and proven health benefits.

+ Encourage the person to take time to grieve.

It is possible for a person to delay his or her grief. This often occurs when someone is forced to help others cope or has important tasks to accomplish. However, some experts believe that the longer the reaction is delayed, the more unhealthy the reaction can eventually be. If you know a disaster survivor who is playing the part of the good soldier or keeping a "stiff upper lip," gently encourage him or her to be fully present and honest with the current situation and loss.

+ Provide opportunities for the person to talk.

Talking about an event releases tears, emotions, and suffering. But this sort of suffering is an important part of healing. People who are isolated and lonely as a result of a disaster desperately need to talk. However, they may not know how to share their deep emotions. They may also be afraid to face the emotions that may surface.

Honestly explain why you want to hear the person's story. Listen to the person intently and actively while reserving judgment or advice.

+ Use language of empowerment and hope.

First, help the disaster survivor find physical safety. Then remind him or her of the reasons he or she is safe and what the person must do to remain so. Help the person avoid attitudes of fear and helplessness, and help the survivor understand that his or her response to the current situation will have a dramatic effect on future experiences. Help the person see the hope that can be realized by taking responsibility now.

WHEN TO REFER

+ The survivor's tendency to withdraw and isolate increases.

After a period of time, the survivor should begin to increase his or her sociability. If this is not the case, and he or she seems to be withdrawing even more, it may be time to seek professional help. The increased isolation of the survivor could lead to more serious behavior such as self-neglect, depression, or even suicide.

Ministry Tips

✛ Establish a church referral service.

Call on the goodwill of local churches. Gather those with valuable skills, such as carpenters, electricians, and plumbers, and encourage them to volunteer their time to help rebuild the community. Encourage churches to work together to provide meals, either to individuals or to the community at large. Explain to volunteers that being present to simply listen to survivors' stories is a valuable service.

✛ Rally the troops to "adopt" the survivor.

People suffering isolation in the aftermath of a disaster find it difficult to ask for help. Encourage local churches to "adopt" these survivors and provide the comfort and care they need. One or two families a week can place a phone call, send a card, make a meal, or stop by for a visit. This will provide the survivor with the human contact needed, without the pressure of having to seek it out.

✛ Take the survivor through the truths of Scripture.

A person who has lost his or her support system in a disaster may have a difficult time seeing anything but darkness and negativity. Take a moment to read aloud Psalm 23 or Psalm 34 together. Pause occasionally to discuss what the verses are saying, what they mean to you, and what they mean to the survivor. Help ingrain the truths of Scripture into the survivor's thoughts; they can become a source of comfort after a disaster. If the survivor doesn't have a Bible or has lost it in the disaster, make sure to provide one.

What Not to Say

+ "At least you didn't lose..."

Things could always be worse, and it's natural to try to help people to be positive. Even if the loss of the person you're helping might seem comparatively small considering what others have lost, it still is life changing for the disaster survivor. Remember that even the loss of a landmark, restaurant, or building may have a profound effect on a disaster survivor. The survivor is actually grieving the loss of a sense of security, safety, and peace he or she had before the disaster.

+ "I know how you feel...I understand."

Unless you have been in a similar situation and have experienced a similar loss, you *don't* understand. And even if you have had a similar experience, now is not the time to share your horror stories. Now is the time to listen and be supportive.

+ "Your loved one is in a better place."

Using clichés like this tends to minimize the pain that a survivor is going through. The truth may be that the deceased is indeed in better place, but to the survivor, the pain resides in the fact that the loved ones are no longer here with them.

What to Say

+ "I wish I could take your pain away."

This statement lets the person know you acknowledge his or her pain and that you want to help. The survivor needs to know that what he or she is feeling is normal and it's OK to hurt, thus bringing freedom to grieve in a healthy manner.

+ "You are not alone in this."

Be available to listen when the survivor is ready to talk. Checking in on the person on a regular basis can assure him or her that you are there to help, and that you are planning to be supportive as long as you are needed.

+ "Tell me about your loss."

Allow disaster survivors to talk openly about the people, pets, or possessions they have lost. Mourning the loss helps survivors hold on to the memories. The stories may be repeated over and over and for weeks and months on end. Be patient and listen. This is part of the process and will help the survivor to eventually let go. Don't feel like you have to respond or ask questions. Your presence will speak volumes.

SCRIPTURE HELP

+ **Deuteronomy 31:6**
+ **Psalm 18:28**
+ **Psalm 23:4**
+ **Isaiah 41:10**
+ **John 8:12**

+ **John 14:1**
+ **Romans 8:38-39**
+ **Romans 15:13**
+ **Hebrews 13:5b**

ADDITIONAL RESOURCES

+ Books

Cornils, Stanley P. *The Mourning After: How to Manage Grief Wisely.* Saratoga, CA: R&E Publishers, 1990.

Price, Eugenia. *Getting Through the Night: Finding Your Way After the Loss of a Loved One.* New York: Dial Press, 1982.

Wright, H. Norman. *Helping Those Who Hurt.* Minneapolis, MN: Bethany House Publishers, 2003.

Yancey, Philip. *Where Is God When It Hurts?* Grand Rapids, MI: Zondervan, 1977.

CHAPTER TEN

Multifaith and Unchurched Survivors
Knowing How to Help

The following story represents the experience of ministry workers who provided comfort and care to a young man whose wife had recently been killed in an automobile accident. The man had been unchurched for many years, and the wife had been raised in a family who adhered to a blend of other religious beliefs.

The call came in about 3 in the afternoon that there was an accident out on Highway 24 involving a young family. The husband was driving his pickup truck with some furniture in the back, and his wife and two young children were following in an SUV close behind. As the two vehicles continued down the road, Dirk would occasionally glance to his side-view mirror to see Melanie on her cell phone in the family car not far behind. As they approached the crest of a hill, Melanie reached over to adjust the CD player, and the hulky SUV started to swerve gently to the right onto the shoulder of the road. Sensing the tires leaving the pavement, Melanie abruptly looked back up to the road and turned the wheel sharply to the left. The SUV veered and caught the uneven edge of the pavement.

In what seemed like an instant, Melanie lost control of the vehicle, and she, with her little boy and girl seat-belted in the back, tumbled and rolled five or six times before settling upside down on the highway median. One minute Dirk could see his family, and the next minute, they were gone from sight. He turned the pickup truck around and raced back to discover his worst nightmare: His family was trapped in an upside-down vehicle.

The family was transported by life-flight helicopter to the nearest hospital. Melanie did not survive the accident. Both children sustained multiple injuries and were in serious condition in the pediatric intensive care unit. Two ministry workers, who had known the family well from where Dirk and Melanie lived, rushed to the hospital.

One of the workers, Bob, had been raised in the church all his life and possessed a deep and vibrant faith in Christ. Greg had come to know Christ later in life and had spent almost 10 years in the military before coming to work at Dirk's company. Greg had been to the Middle East on a few deployments and married his wife while he was stationed in Japan.

As the two workers came to the hospital, both had tremendous sorrow and compassion for Dirk as he sat in the hospital waiting area. Both wanted to share how faith in Christ can make a huge difference in coping with personal catastrophe. Bob's approach was very polite and helpful. Over the course of about an hour, he listened, offered hope, read a verse of Scripture, and prayed with Dirk there in the waiting room. And right after he prayed that God would comfort and bless this hurting family, Dirk thanked him for coming and offering the support. The awkward silence that followed influenced Bob's decision that it was time to leave. Although both ministry workers came together to the hospital, Greg decided to stay a little longer, while Bob gave Dirk a big hug and left.

Greg's approach was a little different. He did not offer a lot of advice or read any verses. He knew that Dirk needed help right now with simple decision-making. He went to ask the nurse if a private room could be arranged for Dirk to be with his children when they came out of surgery. He went to the cafeteria to get Dirk something hot to drink while they waited. Greg returned calls for Dirk from family friends and relatives and gave them updates.

Greg stayed at the hospital with Dirk until midnight. Sometime after 10 p.m., the little girl came out of surgery and was moved into a private room.

As things were getting quieter in the hospital wing, Dirk asked Greg, "Why are you still here?"

"What do you mean?" Greg asked. Dirk simply wondered why Greg didn't do his "chaplain thing" and return home like Bob had done. In a direct yet polite way, Greg replied, "Look, we don't know each other real well except from work. Today is the most devastating day of your life, and you can think of Bob and me as a ministry team some other time. But for now, I would like you just to think of me as one other human being helping another human being, so that I can serve as your friend tonight to help you through this. When family and other friends come to see you, I'll step back and help you in other ways. Would that be OK with you, Dirk?"

"Sure, I guess that'll work," Dirk replied. And over the course of the next few weeks, as the children were later released from the hospital, and a funeral service was held with people coming from all over the country to visit, Greg continued his ministry of comfort to his friend.

Since Melanie's family included some Jewish relatives, Greg and Bob asked permission from their pastor and arranged to include a local rabbi to pray and offer some comforting words during the service at the funeral home. Dirk's life changed so much in the weeks that followed, he decided to change jobs and move back to where his parents lived in another state.

About three months later, Greg received a short note from Dirk indicating how much it meant to have his help in those dark days after the accident. Dirk also noted that he was much closer to God now, thanks to Greg's authentic ministry that helped foster the change in his heart.

Care and Counseling Tips

THE BASICS

Whether you're dealing with an individual family crisis or a major disaster, most people will react with a universal shock and sadness at their circumstances. Their normal world has collapsed, possibly including their structures, daily routines, people networks, and vital resources. Because of the sudden nature of any disaster, even the most stalwart can benefit from the pastoral care and counseling of aid workers.

+ Make no assumptions. As an aid worker, you'll likely encounter people whose responses are complex, influenced by cultural history and rooted in varying religious beliefs. They may have no particular beliefs, or if they ascribe to a religion or worldview different from your own, they may not be open to your views and values. They may assume you are only trying to help them so that they will convert to your faith beliefs. You want to assure them with candor that you are there to help them recover from the tragedy, first and foremost.

+ Offer comfort. Remember that an important element of the aid we offer is God's comfort. In the Bible, Paul summarized this concept: "God is our merciful Father and the source of all comfort. He comforts us in all our troubles so that we can comfort others. When they are troubled, we will be able to give them the same comfort God has given us" (2 Corinthians 1:3b-4).

The very origin of the word *comfort* suggests that our being with other people to comfort them promotes their strength (*comfort*: from the Latin: con + fortis, meaning "with strength").

+ God's love flows through you. What makes the aid we offer distinctly Christian is the fact that our presence with victims is evidence of how God is present with us. The spiritual bond we have with God fosters genuine compassion and allows us to share our own story of faith. That bond is felt by the recipients of our aid, even though they may view life differently.

Beyond the message of encouragement and comfort, the message of Christianity clearly offers hope in the midst of pain and suffering, helping those who suffer to find renewal in life's difficult circumstances. Jesus' own death on the cross and his resurrection show how God redeems our past, transforms our present, and brings courage in the face of any situation.

Remember that it's God's goodness in you that is touching the lives around you. Your life that has been changed by Jesus is also the life that blesses others. No matter what form of care you bring in a crisis, it is an outflow of the gift of God's love through you.

+ Respect beliefs other than your own. It's not uncommon to meet families where there is a mixture of different faith traditions. It may be only slight differences, as with Christians in differing denominations. Sometimes families develop a blend of religious traditions, perhaps Christian and Jewish, Buddhist, or Muslim. The blend of traditions reflects the most common denominator among the family members, and the results may spark some curiosity or even confusion for those outside the family.

As a general principle, be supportive of traditions and allow a measure of grace to compensate for actions that may be outside your range of beliefs. Remember that their actions make complete sense to them, and these actions can later ignite insightful conversations, once the crisis has diminished.

+ Expect different reactions. What kinds of reactions can you expect to find? Some people choose to express their reactions outwardly and others inwardly. Outward expressions may include excessive talking, shouts of frustration, crying, and acting out in anger. Inward expressions include holding back visible emotions, internal wrestling with emotion, withdrawal to a solitary place, or a silent, blank stare into the distance. There is no common reaction to a crisis, as everyone finds his or her own unique expression in the moment.

Care Tips

During the period when the shock of the crisis is still fresh with those you are assisting, the following ideas can help.

+ Remain calm.
Stay calm and allow for emotional reactions. Victims of a disaster or crisis are rarely at their best. Make allowances, and keep your voice even and your actions comforting.

+ Stay safe.
If you are at the scene of a disaster, take precautions to protect yourself from injury or exposure to harmful elements. If possible, or in cooperation with rescue and recovery personnel, assist others in evacuating the area to a safe location before continuing with the care you are to provide.

+ Minimize trauma exposure.
Try to insulate people from the noise and activities of emergency workers. There is a fascination that all people have with staring at an accident scene or disaster site. But it reduces a person's psychological trauma if the person can minimize exposure to such a shocking scene.

+ Be prepared with correct information.
Initially, the aid provided during a disaster response meets the survivors' immediate needs for food, water, shelter, and medical treatment. Following this, people are desperate to communicate their status to extended family members using cell phones or radios. Because you are a helper, people will assume you know important information. Therefore, before you go into a crowd to help, know the location and procedures for helping people find that immediate aid quickly.

✛ Stick to the facts.

Survivors will often present a series of questions, seeking amplifying information. Keep your answers brief, and stick with the facts as you know them. If you do not know the answers to the questions, be honest and say so, along with an assurance that you will work to find answers or put them in contact with someone who can supply such information.

✛ Allow emergency workers to do their jobs.

If you are providing care to an individual or a single family, whether in a waiting area or treatment facility, give preference to visits or calls from police, fire, and medical personnel. Let the emergency workers get what information they require, and then lend your support as time allows.

✛ Be alert to opportunities for contact.

Make use of the long periods of waiting in lines, which can lead to brief conversations of care and encouragement. In July 2006, this kind of care was very successful when aid workers assisted more than 14,000 Americans evacuating Beirut, Lebanon during a border clash between Muslim factions of Lebanon and Israel.

✛ Be sensitive.

Notice those details in a person's overall appearance that are out of the ordinary. For example, provide a blanket or wrap for someone with torn clothing. If that person is dirty, get him or her to a cleaning station or restroom to wash his or her hands and face. A chair or a sleeping cot may also be of help.

✛ Respect religious differences.

Respect differences. "Major on the majors and minor on the minors," as the saying goes. You may encounter varied religious expressions, so it's hard to anticipate what actions may be appropriate.

Those with strong family relationships may engage in a significant amount of physical contact, such as hugging and holding hands. Those who practice the Jewish faith may make a small tear or cut in their clothing as a sign of mourning and grief. They may also hang black cloth over mirrors in the home. Others may light a candle or burn incense as a symbol of constant intercessory prayer.

+ Be patient.

The experienced aid worker knows to exercise both patience and sensitivity when counseling. Be careful to keep language simple (avoiding church jargon or technical words), and wait for an appropriate moment to address personal or spiritual matters so that a sense of privacy and trust is established.

+ Be available to pray.

If you observe a time of prayer with the family, allow them to pray in their own way. One option is to begin the prayer with a short moment of silence to allow them to pray in their own way. When you lead others in prayer, keep the prayer brief and focused on the present moment, using care not to use your prayer as a means to convey your differing theological perspective. You are there to build bridges of goodwill and later will use those connections to discuss elements of faith.

+ Contact clergy.

Offer to assist the family in notifying a local clergy or practitioner of their particular faith. By facilitating this important detail for them, you increase your integrity not only with the family but also in your cooperation with local clergy. If the family has no religious background, of if they have left a church, they will still probably be amenable to your genuine offer of support. Once they have developed more trust in you, they are likely to discuss with you their views on how they have developed a life apart from a spiritual community.

Counseling Tips

✛ Give individuals the time to process the tragedy in their world.

It may be too early to accomplish helpful, on-scene counseling. Don't expect to have lengthy conversations with people. Instead, it is more realistic to have a few brief conversations that build on previous encounters. After a few positive interactions, people will engage with you more to discuss more involved matters. Leave a calling card or contact information with the person or family so they can initiate a follow-up when they are ready.

✛ Reassure victims that such events are beyond the coping ability of anyone.

Their feeling of devastation is understandable. Give them a sense that this is an abnormal situation, and nothing can prepare people for this. Listen for clues in their speech patterns to help you in assessing their need for professional help with a mental health provider. Such clues include disorientation of time and place, dizziness, imbalance, and talk of suicide or vengeance.

✛ Maintain a positive perspective, but be careful not to appear too optimistic in a "Pollyanna" style.

It's common to hear comments of pessimism and sarcasm, but avoid the temptation to join them by talking negatively about other aid workers, complaining, or blaming agencies for their delays or inability to provide adequate support. Look for ways to focus the conversation toward resources they have available right now to make the most out of this desperate situation.

Ministry Tips

Remember that all people matter to God, regardless of their particular faith or even lack of it. Your role is to emulate the very best of what the Christian faith has to offer for someone who has lost all hope.

✛ Rebuild. Work on helping victims rebuild the life they once had. The repair and rebuilding process is the most opportune time to discuss rebuilding the inner spiritual life, as well as the outer physical one.

Equip the person or people to network with others and form an affinity group of some sort—it may be neighbors, co-workers, support groups, or referral organizations. It is important that you help them start some new connections.

✛ Trust. Trust that God has a plan for this person or family. If a family member has a Christian faith and the spouse does not, be careful that your spiritual conversation is not seen as a gang-pile on the unbeliever. That turns discussions into arguments quickly. At some point, it may be better to talk about spiritual matters one-on-one with the unbelieving spouse.

✛ Listen. At times, you'll meet families that share a common faith in God but for whatever reasons have left a church community. The issues here are not really about unchurched beliefs but are better described as de-churched. In cases like this, it may be helpful to listen to the pain and misunderstanding that have precipitated the situation, and consider referring the matter to a clergy or counselor who is assisting in the relief effort or crisis response.

When all is said and done, what really matters is not so much what the people you're helping think of you, but what they learned about God. They may forget you, but they may remember the goodness of God shown through you. Your labor of love among them should set a good Christian example, as the Bible says in Titus 2:7: "And you yourself must be an example to them by doing good works of every kind. Let everything you do reflect the integrity and seriousness of your teaching."

If discussions about religious differences devolve into arguments, consider a waiting period to cool emotions, or refer the person to your team supervisor for the best follow-up contact. Very rarely do people get argued into the kingdom of God. Rather they are led by love and grace.

SCRIPTURE HELP

+ **Psalm 133**
+ **Lamentations 3:22**
+ **Matthew 6:34**
+ **John 14:27**
+ **Romans 5:3**

+ **2 Corinthians 1:3, 4**
+ **Philippians 4:4-7**
+ **Titus 3:1**

What Not to Say

✛ Don't try to explain God's relationship to the disaster.

When dealing with a crisis, it's likely that a person will ask you why God has done such a terrible thing, where God is in all of this, if this is a punishment from God, or if it is a sign of the tribulation. Unless you are a well-known, respected biblical scholar or acclaimed theologian, avoid trying to answer such questions. They are questions that really only God can answer.

One of the best answers you can give is that we may not know why this has happened, but God is very present with us in the moment and truly understands what it is like for us to suffer all kinds of trials and calamities. All that you can do now is to say, "When a crisis happens, I may not know the *why*, but I do know *what* to do. I know to trust in God and rely on the faith that has sustained me through every situation."

✛ "I've been in worse situations. This could be a lot worse."

For the victim of a disaster, this *is* the worst experience, and your prior experiences are not the issue when helping others.

✛ Don't lose your temper and say things you will regret later.

Be careful not to use profanity or terms that could be misunderstood. If there is a language barrier, it helps immensely if you can include local terms that people understand.

✛ Don't make jokes or use morbid humor in the presence of disaster victims.

Immature aid workers may resort to dark humor as a hidden coping behavior because they are overwhelmed or feel inadequate to the task. If you notice this activity, ask the offending aid worker to take a break and get some recovery time so he or she can correct this bad habit. The victims have lost their sense of humor and will only be annoyed with such antics.

+ Never lie.

Offer only those facts you know to be true. Disaster victims are making critical family decisions based on what you say, and even if you are the lowest ranking member on a response team, your words will be taken as a voice of authority.

WHEN TO REFER

+ When a person becomes disruptive.

When a person you are trying to help completely obsesses on a detail, picks on you, or harasses you to the point that it prevents you from doing your work or jeopardizes the safety of yourself or others, it's time to get help from the security or medical personnel in the area to have the person evaluated for mental health issues. Understand that a life crisis can often bring out the worst behavior in people.

+ When the help you offer just isn't enough.

Refer others for counseling or assistance whenever you find yourself in a situation that is simply beyond your ability to offer improvement or to resolve. The type of referral may be to a qualified professional, to a local support group meeting in the area, or to an agency that provides specialized service or support.

What to Say

+ "Even though our beliefs may differ, if it's OK with you, I would just like to help in any way possible, as simple as one person helping another. We can choose to talk about faith later, but for now, let's choose to work with each other to improve this present situation."

This shows you genuinely care for the person's well-being and will try to be as authentic as possible in the delivery of aid or assistance.

+ "I am not here to start an argument. I prefer we start a friendship. Do you think there is a chance we can work together in that space of friendship and respect?"

When you recognize differences but still choose to cooperate on a plan of action, it shows spiritual maturity and courage to those you're helping. They realize you've made a life choice, but there is still room in your life to accommodate their differences. It also conveys that you intend to show respect for their beliefs, and that is a good start for a relationship.

+ "I'm glad you noticed that we have made different choices with respect to our faith in God."

This isn't pushy; it just acknowledges the reality. You could follow with, "It's not something I choose to hide, and it is a reason I enjoy helping others. Our deeply held beliefs drive our choices in life. Perhaps this will be a topic where we can learn a lot from each other in the future."

+ "If you notice that something I say or do sparks your curiosity, feel free to ask me about it."

This kind of statement offers survivors more control in terms of what they want to know about your faith and when they want to know it. If they do ask, it will be out of genuine interest, and you'll be in a position to share your faith as a response to how it can specifically affect their situation.

CHAPTER ELEVEN

Disaster Response Gear Checklist

The Salvation Army suggests using the following checklist before responding to a disaster site.

Packing
- ❏ luggage bag that can be lifted and carried without help
- ❏ suitcases (lightweight with wheels)
- ❏ backpack (for travel and on-site use)

Personal
Clothing sufficient for 7 to 10 days
Spiritual caregivers should carefully consider the appropriateness of their attire at a disaster scene. Caregivers working indoors, or those who will be participating in formal ceremonies such as funerals or remembrance services, should wear their formal ministerial attire. However, caregivers assigned to the field may dress less formally and in fashions similar to other volunteer disaster workers. In addition to being more appropriate to the scene, this will help caregivers blend in with other responders and make them more approachable to disaster survivors and other rescue workers. Even in less

formal attire, however, caregivers should be clearly identifiable as emotional and spiritual care providers and, if they represent a specific denomination, their clothing should also be marked with the emblem of their faith.

- ❏ shirts (8 or 9), preferably marked according to organization
- ❏ hat, preferably marked according to organization
- ❏ comfortable pants with pockets (3 to 4 pairs)—cargo hiking pants are ideal (think fabric that will dry easily)
- ❏ 10 to 12 pairs of socks and underclothing
- ❏ jacket (appropriate to climate), preferably marked according to organization
- ❏ rain poncho
- ❏ comfortable, durable shoes (hiking boots are good)
- ❏ light pajamas
- ❏ jeans
- ❏ extra casual shirts
- ❏ shorts (2 pairs)
- ❏ formal ministerial attire (at least 1 set) for formal ceremonies

Toiletries sufficient for 7 to 10 days

- ❏ contacts/glasses (extra pair of contacts)
- ❏ toothbrush/toothpaste and breath mints
- ❏ deodorant
- ❏ soap and shampoo (may or may not be available where you stay)
- ❏ pain reliever
- ❏ Imodium
- ❏ allergy medicine
- ❏ sewing kit
- ❏ sunscreen
- ❏ bug spray
- ❏ shaving gear
- ❏ personal first aid kit, including adhesive bandages and antibacterial cream
- ❏ individual personal items as needed

Work

- ❑ multiple pens
- ❑ 2 or 3 permanent markers (like Sharpies)
- ❑ 4 or 5 small flip notebooks (for pocket) and 2 or 3 larger spiral notebooks (for note-taking)
- ❑ file folders with pockets (for document storage)
- ❑ business cards
- ❑ valid organizational ID badge with lanyard
- ❑ magnetic signs or window decals to identify your vehicle as part of your organization
- ❑ your own Bible
- ❑ devotional materials to give to others (Choose material that is small and easy to carry. Remember to be thoughtful as to how this material is distributed.)
- ❑ other items to give out (Candy and snacks are good "boosters" for adults; candy, gum, and small books or toys are useful to reach out to children. *Be aware of choking hazards and food allergies—ask parents or caretakers before giving a child anything edible, and ask adults about allergies before sharing food items.*)

Miscellaneous

- ❑ sufficient petty cash—at least several hundred dollars in cash
- ❑ granola bars/cracker packs—bring a few and buy some when you get to the site
- ❑ buy bottled water when you get to the site
- ❑ sunglasses with band
- ❑ alarm clock (Make sure it's reliable, and set two alarm clocks if there's an extra available where you're staying—there will be early mornings.)
- ❑ multiple resealable gallon-sized bags (useful for keeping gear organized)
- ❑ small towel (for car, etc.)
- ❑ wallet/ID/credit card (bring spare photocopies in case originals are lost)
- ❑ flashlight and extra batteries

Technology

- ❏ cellular phone with wall and car charger (include extra batteries if available)
- ❏ GPS unit and car charger
- ❏ laptop computer (Laptops may not always be necessary, but many professionals rely heavily on them for day-to-day business. If you bring a computer, be sure it has wireless Internet access and has both a wall and car charger. Bring a USB flash storage drive plug-in with lanyard for easy exchange of data.)
- ❏ digital camera (Be sensitive to how you use the camera, and maintain the privacy of disaster survivors you're working with.)

OTHER THINGS TO REMEMBER

Before you leave, book...

- ❏ an airline ticket if necessary (one-way)
- ❏ housing (Determine if lodging will be in a hotel or "rougher" conditions, such as staff shelter in a tent, gymnasium, or church. If such hardship accommodations are being utilized, bring at least a sleeping bag. If you have extra space, include a cot, air mattress, and/or extra blankets and pillows.)
- ❏ a rental car

Also remember...

- ❏ to take care of any bills, rent, pet issues, etc., before you leave town
- ❏ to set up an emergency contact person with whom you can communicate (This lets you receive urgent messages from home and lets someone there know where you'll be and how you're doing. This is especially important if communications will be limited.)
- ❏ to keep petty cash and personal cash separate (this helps avoid confusion when submitting expenses)

Fresh, Meaningful Resources
for your **Small Group Ministry!**

Emergency Response Handbook for Small Group Ministry
This rapid-response handbook gives you and your small group the
confidence to share God's love and comfort with hurting friends.

Hope Lives: A Journey of Restoration
Compassion changes everything: how you view the world...yourself...
even Jesus.

Outflow: Outward-Focused Living in a Self-Focused World
Here is your field guide to letting God's love fill you with joy that flows
from you to your family, friends, neighbors. . .your world.

Order today! Visit group.com or call 1-800-447-1070.

Incredible things will happen®

group.com